DOG
FACTS

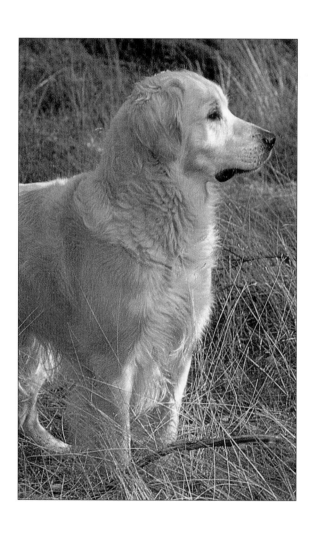

DOG FACTS

JOAN PALMER

FALL RIVER PRESS

This 2009 edition published by Fall River Press,
by arrangement with Quantum Publishing.
6 Blundell Street
London
N7 9BH

Senior Editor Susanna Clarke
Art Editor Anita Ruddell
Designers Hazel Eddington, Frances Austen
Illustrator John Francis
Other Illustrators David Kemp, Sandra Pond, Will Giles
Picture Manager Joanna Wiese
Art Director Nick Buzzard
Publishing Director Janet Slingsby

Fall River Press
122 Fifth Avenue
New York, NY 10011

ISBN: 978-1-4351-1182-0

Printed and bound in Singapore

10 9 8 7 6 5 4 3 2 1

CONTENTS

Section 1

THE NATURE OF THE DOG

When Did Dogs Originate? 8 • Who Domesticated the Dog? 10 • Were Dogs Always Popular? 12 • Have Any Breeds Disappeared? 14 • Rare and Unusual Dogs 16 What is a Pure Breed? 18 • What are Crossbreeds? 19 • What is a Certificate of Pedigree? 20 Are Pedigree Dogs Show Dogs? 22 • Are Dogs Intelligent? 24 Can Dogs Perform Useful Tasks? 26 • Can Dogs Love? 28 • Where Can I Get a Dog? 30 Getting Ready for Your New Pet 32 • Giving Your Dog a Proper Diet 34 House-Training 36 • Training Your Dog 38 • Can I Learn How to Show My Dog? 40 Grooming Your Dog 42 • Exercising Your Dog 44 • Should I Play With My Dog? 46 Will My Dog Show Aggression? 47 • Will My Dog Bark? 48 • Dogs and Vacations 50 Inoculations and Health Care 52 • Canine Disorders 54 • Should I Have My Dog Neutered? 56 What if I want My Dog to Breed? 57 • The Bitch in Whelp 58 • Weaning and Home-Finding 59 How Long Will My Dog Live? 60 • Care of the Elderly Dog 61

Section 2

DOG BREEDS

Breeds of the World Introduction 64 • The Dog Classifications: Groups 66 • The Poodle 72 The Shar-Pei 74 • The Chow Chow 75 • The Schnauzer 76 • The French Bulldog 78 The Dalmatian 79 • The Japanese Spitz 80 • The Bernese Mountain Dog 82 The Rottweiler 84 • The Great Dane 86 • The Doberman 88 • The Siberian Husky 90 The Newfoundland 92 • The Mastiff 93 • The Boxer 94 • The St. Bernard 96 The Komondor 98 • The Old English Sheepdog 99 • The Welsh Corgi 100 The German Shepherd 102 • The Border Collie 104 • The Griffon 106 • The Affenpinscher 108 The Chinese Crested Dog 109 • The Yorkshire Terrier 110 • The Pomeranian 112 The Miniature Pinscher 113 • The Pekingese 114 • The Cavalier King Charles Spaniel 116 • The Chihuahua 118 • The Italian Grayhound 120 • The Airedale Terrier 122 • The Norfolk Terrier 124 • The Bull Terrier 126 • The Staffordshire Bull Terrier 128 • The West Highland White Terrier 130 • The Setters 132 The Weimaraner 134 • The Water Spaniel 136 • The Golden Retriever 138 The Labrador Retriever 140 • The Cocker Spaniel 142 • The Foxhound 144 The Beagle 146 • The Irish Wolfhound 147 • The Bloodhound 148 • The Basenji 150 The Afghan Hound 151 • The Dachshund 152 • The Grayhound 154

Index 156
Credits 160

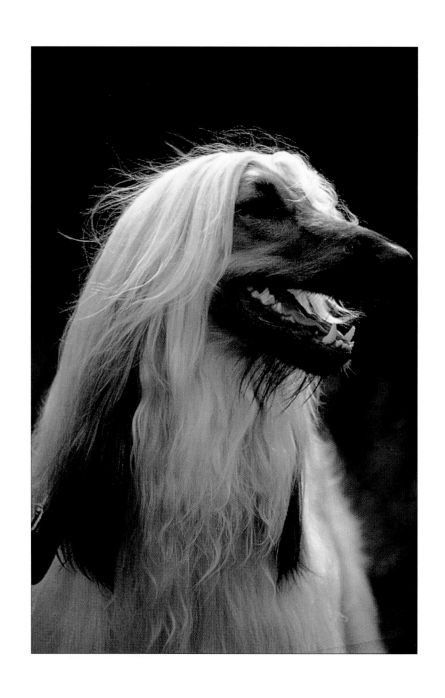

THE
NATURE
OF THE
DOG

When Did Dogs Originate?

The dog, in common with wolves, foxes, and jackals, belongs to the family Canidae. This is one of seven families in the Carnivore, or meat-eating, order of mammals.

The evolution of the dog, *Canis familiaris*, traces back to a small, tree-climbing, weasel-like carnivore, the miacis, which dwelt in forests 50 million years ago. A descendant of the miacis was the tomarctus, a small, fox-like creature, which appeared some 35 million years later and is generally acknowledged as the forerunner of the dog, wolf, fox, and jackal. But the tomarctus had disappeared by the middle of the Pleistocene age, about one million years ago, and by then, wolves and jackals were well established.

"WOLF IN SHEEP'S CLOTHING"

The saying that "a dog is a wolf in sheep's clothing" is not far amiss. The most likely ancestor of the domestic dog is the gray wolf, with which it shares various characteristics. The jackal is another possibility. However it is unlikely that the dog could have evolved from the fox. It is of interest that matings between a wolf and dog prove fertile—as do some between dog and jackal—and that the dog which escapes into the wild will revert to the wolf-like behavior of its ancestors. Much of the behavior patterns of the domestic dog today, particularly when in the company of its own kind, can be traced back to that of the wolf pack.

The dog family is often divided into two distinct groups: the dogs and the wolves, and the foxes and

Miacis

The genus Canis includes the wolf, jackal, and fox, all of which were present in Europe, Asia, and Africa in the Pliocene age 10 million years ago. They appeared in North America only one million years ago.

Tomarctus

The forerunner of miacis, the tomarctus, would appear from its skull to have been similar to the modern dog. It was capable of speed, resembled the badger, and had a red coat and thick tail.

Left: The Egyptian god Anubis, ruler of the dead, was symbolized by both the dog and the jackal. This mythological son of Osiris, god of the underworld, shows a remarkable resemblance to the Pharaoh Hound. It may be seen in the Louvre, Paris. The Pharaoh Hound breed has changed little in 5,000 years.

Right: The jackal (*Canis aureus*), a gregarious species, is renowned for its piercing wail. It is smaller than the wolf, bigger than the fox, and originates in tropical Asia. Crossbreedings of dogs with jackals have been claimed.

jackals. Both have much in common. They are meat-eaters with 42 teeth. They have four or five toes on their forefeet, four on their hindfeet. They run on their toes, and their claws, unlike those of the cat, are non-retractable. The females have a 63-day gestation period. They give birth to fairly large liners, and the eyes of their young are closed at birth. It is also significant that members of these groups live in packs and respect a pack leader. This fact would explain why the domestic dog readily accepts the dictates of a human owner. The owner has become a substitute pack leader!

DOGDOM BC

The earliest identifiable remains of a purebred dog are those of a Saluki, a breed which took its name from the town of Saluk in the Yemen. Recent excavations of the Sumerian civilization in Mesopotamia, dated to 7000BC, revealed rock carvings of dogs bearing a strong resemblance to the Saluki, the original ancestor of which is thought to have been a small-skulled desert wolf. The earliest domesticated dog in recorded history is the Pharaoh Hound; two hounds hunting gazelle are depicted on a circular disk dating back to around 4000BC. The elegant and graceful Pharaoh Hound is known to have played an integral part in the daily lives of the kings of ancient Egypt.

However, while hounds such as the Saluki and Pharaoh the Hound lay claim to being the oldest purebred dogs on Earth, it is interesting (bearing it in mind that wolves, jackals, and dogs will interbreed under certain conditions) to detect those dogs that still resemble their ancestral equivalents and which have developed according not only to climatic conditions but also to the requirements of their new-found human friends.

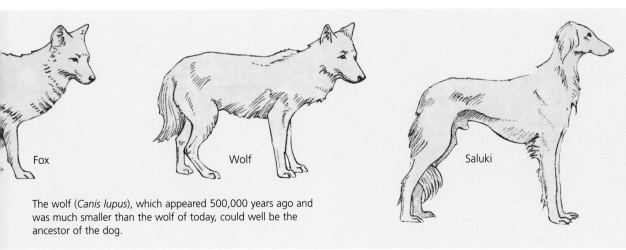

Fox · Wolf · Saluki

The wolf (*Canis lupus*), which appeared 500,000 years ago and was much smaller than the wolf of today, could well be the ancestor of the dog.

9

Who Domesticated the Dog?

It is likely that prehistoric people, realizing they had nothing to fear from the dogs that crept toward their cave or campfire seeking food and warmth, threw them some scraps of meat. The dogs, realizing in turn that humans were not predators, would have crept closer until a bond of companionship and mutual affection developed.

As time went on, humans would have recognized the value of the dog as a guard, beast of burden, sled dog, and hunter, and later would have made the first crude attempts at selective breeding in a desire to perpetuate those traits of conformation, temperament, and ability that they most admired.

Dogs, as we have seen, are descendants of the wolf and it is still possible today to see the result of some of the early attempts at selective breeding. Inuit dogs are by no means dissimilar to the northern races of the wolf. They were frequently crossed with wolves to maintain their size and stamina. The Samoyed is a descendant of the Siberian Wild Dog. Dogs owned by the North American Indians tend to be smaller

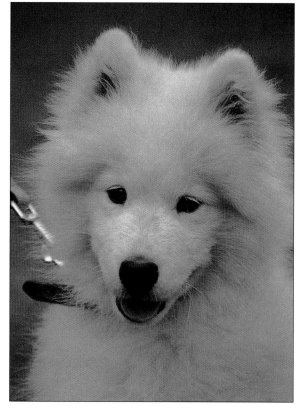

Above: The Samoyed takes its name from the Siberian tribe of Samoyedes. A descendant of the Siberian Wild Dog, it nonetheless "shows affection for all mankind." The explorer Nansen took a number of "Sammies" with him on his expedition to the North Pole. In its native land it guards and protects reindeer.

Left: Despite being reared by a human family, on reaching two or three years of age the Dingo's instinct to live with its own kind becomes stronger than the desire to remain with humans. Some believe it descends from Phu Quoc dogs of eastern Asia that were brought to Australia by seafarers.

DOGGY BONES

In 1979, Israeli archaeologists digging in the Middle East found the remains of a man and a puppy in close proximity. The hand of the man was resting on the puppy. This was among the remains of a 10,000-year-old Natufian settlement!

animals—likely descendants of the coyote or prairie wolf. Of all European dogs, the German Shepherd is certainly the most wolf-like. It was once known as the Alsatian Wolf Dog. Similarities such as these are readily found all over the world. Pariah dogs of India resemble the Indian wolf. Dogs in Africa, Asia, and some parts of southeastern Europe resemble the jackals of those regions, and the Australian dingo also resembles the jackal.

EARLY MAN'S BEST FRIEND

It is apparent that in the early days of domestication, and despite the friendship that had developed between humans and dogs, little or no effort was made to produce anything other than "useful" breeds. The written history of domesticated dogs starts with a work on hunting dogs by Xenophon (c.430–350BC), which was virtually the only significant publication on dogs for over a thousand years. Indeed, it was not until 1685, in Nuremberg, that the first encyclopedia of dogs was published: the *Cynographia Curiosa oder Hundebeschreibung*, by Christian Franz Paullini.

A glimpse, however, of the changing role of the dog to meet social requirements, fashion, and fancy, can be detected in a letter penned in 1560 by the Cambridge scholar, John Caius, to the Swiss naturalist, Gesner, in which he outlined the breeds of dog in England at that time: "And we also have a small race of dogs that are specially bred to be the playthings of rich and noble ladies. The smaller they are, the more perfectly suited to their purpose, which is to be carried at the breast, in the bedchamber, or in the lap, when their mistresses sally forth." Hunting and watchdogs still predominated, but the lap dog had begun to make its mark.

DOG CENSUS

The domestic dog population of the world is estimated to be over 200 million. The United States has the largest population, approximately 62 million. The UK has 6.8 million. But these figures are not all for purebred dogs, of which the United States has around 15 million.

A PACT

The dog is a creature that humans have never had to subdue into subservience, or with which they have

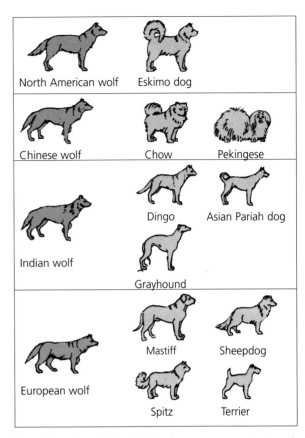

North American wolf | Eskimo dog

Chinese wolf | Chow | Pekingese

Indian wolf | Dingo | Asian Pariah dog | Grayhound

European wolf | Mastiff | Sheepdog | Spitz | Terrier

been forced to do battle, for there are no ancient rock carvings illustrating such situations. It appears that Dog formed an alliance with Man of its own free will, and a partnership was formed on the basis of mutual friendship and trust.

OLDEST BREEDS

• The oldest purebred British dog is reckoned to be the Cardigan Welsh Corgi, which traces back to dogs brought to Wales by the Celts from the Black Sea area in around 1200BC.

• The oldest purebred American breed is the American Foxhound. This dates back to 1650 when Robert Brooke, an Englishman, settled in Maryland, with his pack of foxhounds. These he crossed with other strains imported from England, Ireland, and France, and thus the American Foxhound was developed.

Were Dogs Always Popular?

There have always been dog lovers and dog haters. Rows and rebellion over dog legislation is nothing new. In 1796 there was a motion to introduce the first duties on dogs in England: five shillings on "outdoor" dogs, three shillings on "indoor" dogs. It was proposed by one George T. Clark, who was rewarded for his trouble with the receipt of dozens of dead dogs in hampers, packed as game. There was a massacre of dogs by owners who objected to paying the dues.

On balance, the dog has been more revered than reviled through the ages. The ancient Egyptians are known to have had faithful dogs buried alongside them, a practice also followed in ancient America by the Toltec people, and later by the Aztecs, whose dogs were sacrificed at funerals in the belief that they would guide their masters to a better world.

HOLY DOGS

We know that the dog has played a large part in Eastern religions and that although it is considered by Muslims to be an outcast of Allah, and unclean, the fleet-footed Saluki is still prized along with purebred Arab horses. Hindus believe that a person who ill treats a dog will be punished by returning to Earth in canine form. It is often the fear of the unknown that has made humans behave unreasonably toward animals. Here lies the source of totemism—the identification of themselves by human families with an animal family—and of metempsychosis—the belief in the transmigration of human souls, and their return in an animal's body.

The importance of shepherd dogs and guard dogs was stressed in the teachings of the Persian prophet,

Zoroaster (Zarathustra), almost 3,000 years ago. Zoroaster's doctrine, which spread widely in the East, bore many references to dogs and their importance. He decreed: "If these two dogs of mine, the shepherd dog and the guard dog, pass the house of any of my faithful people, let them never be kept away from it,

Below: While in the East, Muslims scorned the dog, credited with devouring the body of the Prophet Mohammed, fear of the animal was also prevalent in Europe, where the word "dog," or "cur" became an insult.

STARRY DOG

Even in astrology, dogs are a force to be reckoned with and there is more than a little truth in the saying that, "every dog has its day." There are forty "dog days" between 3 July and 11 August, when Sirius, the Dog Star, rises and sets with the Sun. The superstition that Sirius greatly influences the canine race is found in Greek literature, as far back as Hesiod in the eighth century BC.

STATUS DOGS

● Wealth and snobbery have always played their part in dog ownership and, in the time of King Richard I of England, anyone who kept a grayhound, unless he was worth £100 ($586) a year in land or inheritance, or £300 ($17580) a year in freehold, was liable to be summoned to the Forest Court, which met every year to determine whether his grayhound had been running in the forest.

● In the Middle Ages there were reckoned to be no less than 69 royal forests, 800 parks, and 13 chases in England and the comment was frequently made that, if you wanted to see a King of England you need look no further than the hunting field.

● The common people were allowed to keep only watch dogs and small dogs that were incapable of bringing down game and therefore spoiling their betters' sport. Large dogs would be systematically and cruelly lamed.

● To this day there exists in the village of Lyndhurst in the county of Hampshire a measure, or stirrup, through which a dog had to pass so as to assess whether it was sufficiently small to be allowed to roam unhindered in the forest.

for no house could exist, but for these two dogs of mine, the shepherd dog and guard dog."

Dogs were even worshipped by the followers of Mithras, who was aided and accompanied by his dog, and whose cult flourished for almost five centuries in Roman times, spreading from India to Spain and from Egypt to the south of Scotland.

There is a dog-worshipping sect to this day. It is called the Brotherhood of the Essenes. The Essenes maintain that there are animal planes in the celestial kingdom from which one steps to the planes of knowledge. It is their view that animals have power of speech in the kingdom that they relinquish voluntarily as they journey through the gates of the zodiac into Earth's sphere. According to their beliefs, dogs are beings without sin, sent to earth to test humans.

Below: The Saluki is a fleet-footed dog able to keep pace with fast Arab horses. In the Middle East it is still used for hunting the gazelle. Elsewhere it is mainly kept as a lean and elegant pet.

Have Any Breeds Disappeared?

Many dogs have disappeared—some (like the unfortunate "turnspit") into total extinction, others being sacrificed in the development of another, changed variety.

The "turnspit" is, in the words of canine historian, Carson Ritchie, "the best known representative of those worker-dogs which had once provided power for various purposes, such as raising water from a well by working a treadmill." Prior to the introduction of the "turnspit" dog, meat in 18th century England was turned on the spit by a human, usually a small boy, protected from the fierce heat by a round, woven straw shield, soaked in water. However, special treadmills were built near to the fires of large kitchens in great houses and dogs were trained to keep them turning. It would take at least three hours for a large side of beef to roast properly. The dog had to turn the wheel hundreds of times and was subject to beatings from the cook if it paused in its unenviable task. So exhausting was the work that sometimes two "turnspit" dogs were kept, so that one might work on the other's day off. What did the "turnspit" dog look like? They have been described as "extremely bandy legged, so as to appear almost incapable of running, with long bodies and rather large heads. They are very strong in the jaws, and are what is called 'hard bitten'. It is a peculiarity in these dogs that they generally have the iris of one eye black, and the other white. Their color varies, but the usual one is a blueish-gray,

spotted with black. The tail is generally curled on the back." At any rate, this sadly misused little animal was to survive until around 1870, by which time it had become so rare that owners of such treasures were enabled to hire them out by the day. There were also, up until the 19th century, dogs such as the cur, a cross between a sheepdog and a terrier, and the drover's dog, a cross between a sheepdog and a mastiff, the task of which was to guide a farmer's sheep to market. The cur was a watchdog with perhaps less than the social standing of the present day mongrel, and its title had become a derogatory term.

Right: The Bulldog is the breed most generally associated with bull-baiting. It would seize the bull by the nose and hold it until it fell. This unsavory sport was promoted by an Englishman, Earl Warren of Stamford. After watching two dogs fight bulls in 1209 he sought to bring the spectacle to a wider audience. It was made illegal in 1838.

THE QUEEN'S POM

Queen Victoria, an avid lover of most breeds of dogs, became a champion of the Toy varieties, notably, and before the arrival in England of the Pekingese, of the Pomeranian, which initially was a much larger dog weighing as much as 30lb (13.5kg). The Pomeranian was, however, bred down, and by 1896 show classes for the breed had been divided into those for exhibits under and over 8lb (3.5kg) in weight. By 1915 exhibits over that weight had all but disappeared.

Left: "Cave Canem": beware the dog. In ancient Rome, fierce dogs were highly prized, though rarely for their fidelity. They were watchdogs, messengers and combatants. Sometimes they would be starved before meeting their opponents.

15

Rare And Unusual Dogs

As I write, the world's rarest dog is reckoned to be the Tahltan bear dog which, as its name implies, was once used by the Tahltan people of western Canada for bear hunting, and also against lynx and porcupine. It is understood that the Tahltan carried these dogs—the weight of one is around 30lb (13kg)—in hide sacks on their backs, so as to preserve their strength for when the quarry was sighted, at which time they

ON ICE

The Broholmer is a breed recognized only in its native Denmark. It was believed to have become extinct in the 1960s but then, in December 1974, a dog of the breed appeared at the home of a pharmacist in Helsinki, Finland. The Royal Veterinary College in Copenhagen set up a frozen sperm bank for the dog, which was named Bjoern, in the hope that a bitch might eventually be found. But alas, this did not prove to be the case, and Bjoern died in January 1975.

A ROCK DAY

The Lundehund is a breed which for centuries has lived solely on two islands in the north of Norway. Unlike other dogs which have four toes, and possibly an atrophied fifth, the Lundehund has five toes and an atrophied sixth. Also, unlike other small dogs with five toe cushions, the Lundehund has seven or eight. Because of its small size and this strange foot equipment the dog is able to scale rocks and cliffs so as to gently lift a puffin from its nest and restore it unharmed to his master.

would promptly be released. The job of the bear dog was to hold the proposed victim at bay, circling it until its masters moved in for the kill. There are few of the breed now alive and it is in danger of extinction.

This was a fate which threatened the Chinese Shar-Pei and the Chinese Crested Dog not so long ago, and both are now fairly commonplace, particularly in the British show ring.

Right: The Portuguese Warren Hound (pequeño) is usually fawn, but may be yellow, brown, gray-black, or sooty, with or without white patches and spots. It is not currently recognized by the American and United Kingdom Kennel Clubs or the International Canine Federation (FCI).

Below: The Portuguese Water Dog is a very muscular animal. Its toes are webbed to their tips with a soft membrane covered with hair. It may be black, white or various shades of brown; or combinations of black or brown with white.

THE PODENGO

It would indeed be true to say that what is rare today may not be rare tomorrow, so one must hope that the future will be brighter for another breed threatened with extinction, the Portuguese Warren Hound, or Podengo, which is little known outside its country of origin where it is a hunter of rabbit, hare, and deer. There are three sizes of this variety, the grande (large), which stands 22–27in (56–68cm) high, and whose numbers are diminishing, a small variety (pequeño), which resembles a large, smooth-coated Chihuahua, and a medium-sized dog. The grande is not unlike the Ibizan Hound.

THE PORTUGUESE WATER DOG

There is another Portuguese dog which is unusual, albeit not as rare, and that is the Portuguese Water Dog, a fascinating animal, which was once readily seen at Portuguese and Spanish seaports working as a fisherman's dog, guarding the nets. It is remarkable in that it will catch an escaping fish in its jaws and swim back with it to its master.

THE LOWCHEN

The Lowchen, a native French breed, registered in its country of origin under the title, *petit chien lion*, "little lion dog," had all but died out more than 20 years ago, but is now a popular contender in the show ring—though little seen, it must be admitted, being taken for a walk in a park. Believed to have been a favorite of the Duchess of Alba, it is thought that the dog shown with her in a portrait painted by Francisco Goya (1746–1828) is a Lowchen. There is no doubt about the breed in the delightful portrait *A Lowchen Seated by a Quill* painted by Florent Richard De Lamarre between 1630 and 1718, revealing, then as now, the distinctive lion clip which is worn by this delightful member of the Bichon family.

COURT FAVORITES

It is recorded by the famous diarist, Samuel Pepys, that King Charles II spent more time playing with his dogs in the Council Chamber than he did on affairs of state. However, credited as the most fanatical dog lover of all time was Henry III of France (1551–89). Indeed, according to the *Guinness Book of Pet Records* he collected dogs as people collect stamps. When he saw one that took his fancy, and it wasn't for, sale, he would think nothing of arranging for someone to steal it for him. Seemingly he had at least 2,000 dogs spread around his palaces and, when he was in residence, there were never less than 100 dogs, mostly toy breeds, within patting distance. But then the love of Royalty for dogs is well known. Edward VII's faithful Fox Terrier, Caesar, followed his late master's funeral procession, and Slipper, a Cairn Terrier given by Edward VIII to the then Mrs. Wallis Simpson, featured largely in their much publicized courtship correspondence. The present Queen, Elizabeth II, is rarely photographed in home surroundings without a few Corgi dogs beside her.

What is a Pure Breed?

A purebred dog is one whose sire (father) and dam (mother) are of the same breed, the parents having themselves descended from dogs of the same breed. It has been explained how early people would have attempted planned matings of their canine companions so as to perpetuate those traits they admired and desired. They would have experimented with such things as height, weight, and coat type, with color patterns, with the shape of the dog's head and skull, and the setting of its tail until, in the course of a few generations, the desired canine type would breed true.

Doubtless, subsequent dog fanciers would have discussed the attributes of their animals much as people do today. However, while we have the legacy of many paintings which depict breeds of dogs that appear to have changed little from those we know now, it is almost impossible to chart their progress. This is because it was not until 1873 that the Kennel Club in London—the first of its kind in the world—was formed. The Kennel Club introduced a registration system, so that one might determine the breeding of every purebred canine—in what amounted to its own birth certificate—and also refer to an approved "Standard" for each variety of dog that was recognized.

Of course the desire to continue to introduce and improve breeds has continued and there are remarkably few varieties that do not owe their present existence to another breed. The Doberman, for example, owes much to the Rottweiler and Manchester Terrier, and the little Long Coat Chihuahua to the Papillon, or Butterfly Dog, so named because of the shape of its ears.

TALLEST AND SHORTEST

● The tallest dog breeds are the Great Dane, the Irish Wolfhound, the St. Bernard, the English Mastiff, the Borzoi and the Anatolian Karabash (Turkish Shepherd dog). All of these breeds can attain 36in (90cm) at the shoulder.

● The smallest dog breed is the Chihuahua, the recognized weight of which is between 2–6lb (0.9–2.75kg). Mexico City's Natural History Museum, however, has the skeleton of a fully grown Chihuahua measuring only 7in (18cm) in total length. There is no weight quoted for this dog, which was presented in 1910, but it is estimated that if its bones are anything to go by, it could not have weighed more than 1lb (500g).

● The second smallest dog is reckoned to be the Yorkshire Terrier which "officially" should not weigh more than 7lb (3.2kg), but many pet "Yorkies" nowadays tend to be much heavier.

Left: The Grayhound is a pure breed that has not altered materially from its likeness carved in an Egyptian tomb in the Nile Valley c. 4000BC. It has been used for courting since Roman times. Nowadays it is bred along distinct lines for showing, coursing, and track racing.

What are Crossbreeds?

A crossbreed is the progeny of a purebred bitch that has mated with a purebred dog of another pure breed—for example, the result of a Poodle–Spaniel mating.

There are those who favor crossbreeds, believing that they will have the benefit of the attributes of both breeds. In fact, a problem often arises where an owner, having lost a crossbreed of a certain type wishes to replace it with another, for crossbreeds are rarely intentionally bred.

A mongrel is a dog or bitch whose sire and dam are likely to owe their makeup to any number of different breeds.

OLD WIVES' TALE

There is an old wives' tale that mongrels are more robust than purebred dogs. In fact, the mongrel is unlikely to be any tougher or weaker than its purebred contemporaries.

There is no doubt that mongrels make excellent pets but there is always an element of uncertainty as to how they will turn out with regard to either appearance or temperament.

Pure breed of same type = pure breed

Pure breeds of different types = 'X' breed

'X' breed + 'X' breed = mongrel

Above: The result of mating two purebred dogs of different breeds can be successful or somewhat startling, depending on the varieties involved.

Right: Mongrels can have tremendous appeal. Whereas with a purebred pup you can be reasonably sure how it will turn out, with a mongrel you have to take pot luck.

Above: Mongrels come in all shapes and sizes. This example could well have a touch of Boxer in its makeup. White Boxers do sometimes occur, but are not accepted in the show ring. They do, however, make excellent pets.

FEET FIRST

The best way to determine how large a mongrel puppy is likely to grow is to look at the size of its feet. A pup with really large feet is destined to be a mammoth-sized dog.

What is a Certificate of Pedigree?

It is a common mistake to refer to a "pedigree" dog. The correct term is a purebred dog. A Certificate of Pedigree is the document that should be handed to the buyer of a purebred pup at the time of purchase. The buyer should also be given a transfer form enabling him or her, for a modest fee, to register the pup in the buyer's name, in place of the vendor's, with the respective national kennel club. The Certificate of Pedigree which, like the transfer form, should be signed by the breeder, must show the registered name and number of the puppy—obviously you can call your pup whatever pet name you wish—its date of birth, and the registered names and registration numbers of its parents and ancestors for three, or preferably five, generations.

This Certificate of Pedigree is a valuable document which calls for careful scrutiny. Unless the pup's parents are registered, and the signature of the breeder appears, the new owner will be unable to register a transfer of ownership and, perhaps more importantly, will be unable to enter the dog in purebreed show classes, or to register and sell its subsequent progeny as purebred.

You will probably notice on a Certificate of Pedigree that most of the dogs' names bear a prefix, for instance, "Merry Max of Penfold" or "Penfold Merry Max". This is because breeders, again for a modest fee, are enabled to register a prefix with their respective kennel club, which enables stock from their kennels to be easily recognized. Where a dog has been bred by the prefix holder, the word will appear in front of the dog's name (called an affix). If the dog has been acquired, the prefix will follow the dog's name, for example "of" or "at", and this is called a suffix.

HOW TO DETECT PRIZE-WINNING STOCK

If you attend dog shows and look at the catalog entries for a specific breed, you may find it interesting to detect, from their affixes, those kennels that predominate and produce considerable prizewinning

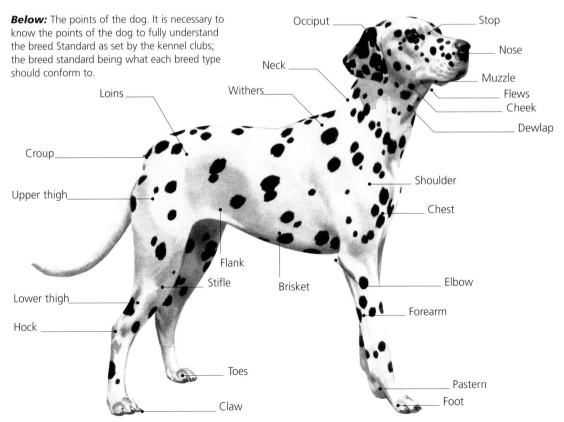

Below: The points of the dog. It is necessary to know the points of the dog to fully understand the breed Standard as set by the kennel clubs; the breed standard being what each breed type should conform to.

Occiput — Stop
Neck — Nose
Withers — Muzzle
Loins — Flews
Croup — Cheek
Upper thigh — Dewlap
Lower thigh — Shoulder
Hock — Chest
Flank — Elbow
Stifle — Forearm
Brisket — Pastern
Toes — Foot
Claw

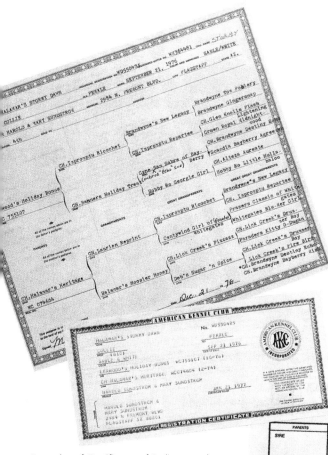

stock. Pedigree certificates are usually completed by hand. Those which have entries written in red ink are highly prized, for only the names of champions are thus honored.

The American and British championship systems are different. In Britain, champions are dogs that have been awarded three Challenge Certificates at three different Championship Dog Shows and by three different judges. In the USA, a championship is attained via an accumulation of points. A dog that has accumulated five points is designated a champion. The dog may earn from one to five points at a show, and only one male and one female can win points a show. It is worth repeating that, when buying a pup, the Certificate of Pedigree warrants careful scrutiny and that even if the pup you intend to buy is an attractive and healthy example of its breed, and you have no intention of exhibiting or breeding from it, if the certificate is incomplete the pup should not command as high a price as its fellows which are correctly documented.

Examples of Certificates of Pedigree and registration documents:
Top: US Pedigree;
Above: American Kennel Club Registration Certificate;
Right: UK Pedigree;
Below right: The UK Kennel Club Registration Certificate.

CHAMPION OF CHAMPIONS

The greatest number of Challenge Certificates, or "CCs" as fanciers call them, to be won by a British dog, were the 78 awarded to champion U'Kwong King Solomon, a Chow Chow owned and bred by Mrs. Joan Egerton of Bramhall, Cheshire, in the north of England. Known as Solly, this magnificent Chow Chow died in 1978 aged 10 years. It is the life's ambition of some dog exhibitors to win even one Challenge Certificate.

Are Pedigree Dogs Show Dogs?

The acquisition of a certificate of Pedigree proves that you own a purebred dog. It enables you to register ownership with the national kennel club, to legitimately enter the animal in purebred show classes and, if you wish to breed, to sell its progeny with a similar Certificate of Pedigree. But—contrary to a widely held belief—a pedigreed dog is by no means always a prospect for the show ring.

FALLING SHORT OF PERFECTION

Kennel clubs worldwide have what is known as a standard laid down for each recognized breed. This standard describes the perfect example of every variety and it is the dogs which meet this exacting requirement that compete against each other in the show ring. There are, however, countless breed members that fall short of their standard of perfection, if only in some minor detail—they may be slightly too big, or too small; their teeth formation may be under- or over-shot, or there could be a wrongful patch of color on their coats—in which case, they would be sold (most purebred dogs are) as "pet" dogs rather than show dogs.

Most people only want an attractive, faithful companion of their favorite breed. However, problems can arise when, having made a purchase, and thinking that their pet is a show dog, they enter it in a show with disastrous results. "But my dog has a Certificate of Pedigree," they then say. "I paid a good price for it. I have been swindled if my dog is not a show dog." But the truth of the matter is that they have been treated fairly, having bought a healthy example of the breed. They never asked the breeder for a show dog.

Obtaining a show prospect is not easy, particularly as it is rarely possible to determine a dog's true potential until it is six months of age, or more. Often breeders will "run-on" a likely pup in their kennels, with a view to exhibiting or breeding from it themselves. A good dog is an advertisement for their kennels!

Those who want to exhibit must first convince a breeder that they will prove to be a worthy owner, and

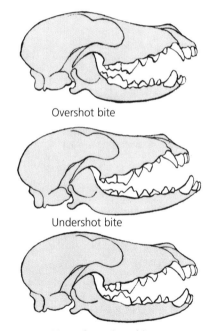

Overshot bite

Undershot bite

Normal or scissor bite

Below and opposite: The correct shape and position of the tail varies according to the breed.

Above: A dog's mouth is overshot when the upper teeth project beyond the lower. It is undershot if the lower jaw projects.

Set high and carried erect (usually docked)

Ring tail, set high

Set high, folded along the back

Set high and carried horizontally, low in repose

Erect ears with medium-high set-on (sometimes cropped)

Bat ears set high and broad at the base

of their keenness to become involved in the breed, probably by joining the relevant breed club, attending many shows as a spectator and learning all they can about handling the variety. Once they have passed this test, and been rewarded with the acquisition of their first show dog, they will discover that the world of show dogs is a completely new way of life.

Pendulous ears, set low

Folded ears, drooping forward

THE SUPREME SHOW

Crufts dog show is the largest dog show in the world. It has been held annually in London since 1886, with the exception of the years 1918–20 and 1940–47, when it was cancelled. When the show was first held at the Royal Aquarium in Westminster, it was restricted to Terrier breeds, but four years later, other groups, including Toys, were added. The Golden Jubilee show held at the Royal Agricultural Hall, Islington, in 1936, attracted record numbers—10,650 entries and 4,388 dogs. However, this was before entry was restricted, as is now the case, to prize-winners in championship shows. The British Kennel Club has run Crufts since 1948, the venue being London's Olympia Halls and subsequently Earls Court Exhibition Centre. However, in January 1991, the show moved to the National Exhibition Centre in Birmingham to celebrate its centenary.

Rose ears, set back

Semi-erect ears

Above right: The size, position, and fall of the ears is also specified in the breed standard.

Right: The Dalmatian's spots should be clearly defined. Those on the extremities should be smaller than those on the body.

Long, set high and carried sickle-like; low in repose

Medium set-on, carried saber-like

Otter tail of medium length, rounded without feather

Long, set low and curved at the tip

Are Dogs Intelligent?

This is a question that scientists have argued over for centuries. We know that dogs are incapable of logical thought as we know it. They cannot reason as we can, but in terms of a "domestic wolf" they are indeed intelligent, relying on association, scent, instinct and memory. They also display characteristics of guarding, loyalty, and playfulness which are typical of the wolf pack and a keen sense of humor.

It is known that pups untouched by human hands during the first weeks of life never become wholly domesticated. Similarly, the dog that is kenneled, fed, groomed, and exercised, but otherwise given little attention, is unlikely to reach the same potential as its contemporary which is kept as a household pet, spoken to regularly, played with, and introduced to any number of outside influences and experiences.

TEACHING YOUR DOG

Dog training must be interpreted by the dog as an extension of play. Learning, however, is largely a matter of association. Some dogs, like some humans, are more intelligent than others, but there are few that given time and having recognized the keywords, will not react to sentences such as: "Shall we (Let's) go for a WALK, Ben," "Goodness, it's time for BED, Ben!," "Do you want your DINNER?," "Here's MUM (or

Above: These curious Jack Russell pups enjoying tug-of-war are having a dress rehearsal for the more serious business of hunting rats and other small vermin.

Dad)!," and "Let's go and meet JANE." The list is endless and the dog's reaction could reasonably be thought to mean that it understands the meaning of the word spoken. It cannot, but associates the keyword, whether or not used in conjunction with its name, with the action that takes place thereafter.

ACTIONS RATHER THAN WORDS

It is not just the spoken word that brings about this association in the canine mind. Actions can speak as loudly as words. The mere fact of a dog's owner walking into the hall, or kitchen, with a coat on may be enough for the dog to jump up from its basket in anticipation of a walk, while the sound of a car engine in the drive may be sufficient to send it running hurriedly to the door in anticipation of its master's arrival. Undoubtedly the more time one spends with one's dog the more it learns, and the more it learns, the more it endears itself to us.

Most pet owners have only one dog. They do not have the same opportunity as those who keep several of studying the behavior of the social pack.

SUBSTITUTE PACK LEADERS

It has been explained how humans became substitute pack leaders, whom our domesticated wolf knows he must respect. Where, however, there are a number of dogs, the biggest, strongest male will generally emerge as the canine pack leader. He will marshal his troops, standing aside, for instance, until all have been accounted for when going out of doors. He will guard the food bowls, sometimes literally forbidding another

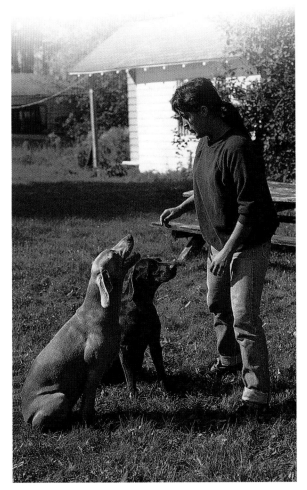

Above: *In a domestic situation the dog regards its human owner as a substitute pack leader. It feels secure in the subordinate role and wants to win the leader's approval.*

MOOD MONITORS

● One of the reasons why dogs bring great comfort to humans is their uncanny facility for picking up on our moods. The dog, in common with its ancestor, the wolf, is sensitive to atmosphere. That is why it will come and sit quietly beside us when we are despondent or jump around enthusiastically when we are in high spirits.

● Dogs have an inbuilt sense of time. How else would they know to draw attention to themselves when a regular feeding time draws near?

● It has also been proved that dogs can recognize places, even if they have not visited them for months, or even years. Indeed, a dog that has been sleeping quietly in the back of a car may get up and show considerable excitement within a half-mile or so of a once familiar location.

dog to eat until he allows it to do so—even, on some occasions, giving an unliked subordinate what amounts to the evil eye until the unfortunate animal creeps away into a corner. Much however depends on the breed and temperament of the dog.

Often there is a second in command, and even a third in pecking order, while some dogs do not aspire to leadership at all. Disagreements are rare except where three important factors raise their head: sex, food, and jealousy.

Can Dogs Perform Useful Tasks?

It is almost impossible to list the many useful tasks that dogs undertake, but there are a few.

There are search and rescue dogs, specially trained to detect missing persons or bodies in an area of scent. They are highly trained dogs, which frequently live the life of family pets when not on call. The dogs go out with their masters, usually skilful hill climbers, in all weathers, and their value is being increasingly recognized in the case of avalanches, aircraft crashes, and earthquakes.

ARMED SERVICE DOGS

There are dogs in the armed services, working for customs and excise and for the police. They are variously used as guards, patrol dogs, and as "sniffer" dogs trained in the detection of explosives and narcotics. Some dogs, particularly the Bloodhound with its incredible scenting ability, are used to track criminals or find lost children.

DOGS THAT "SEE" AND "HEAR"

Perhaps the best known worker dogs are sheepdogs and guide dogs for the blind. However, there are also hearing dogs for the deaf. A "hearing" dog is taught to respond to the sounds chosen by the individual applicant like a knock at the door, the whistle of a kettle, or the ring of a telephone or alarm clock;

Above: Sniffer dogs are on active service in many countries.

Below: Hearing dogs for the deaf have proved so successful that dogs are being trained for other disabilities.

IT SEEMS LIKE PLAY

Work must always be interpreted by a dog as play. When an RAF "sniffer" dog is being trained, his reward is to retrieve. When a young dog retrieves a package of cannabis he will be allowed to have a game with the package, but that will be the only game he is allowed when working.

A dog's instincts are channeled into retrieving a particular scent. The dog gets every individual scent and breaks it down in its head until it finds the one that it knows its master desires, regardless of what else is with it. The dog builds up a "scent picture." Every picture given to the dog includes the drug or explosive that the dog has been trained to find as a common denominator.

happenings that would go undetected by the deaf person were it not for the help of their dog in drawing attention to them.

DOGS FOR PETTING

There are assistance dogs for the disabled also trained to answer their needs, and Pro-Dogs Active Therapy Dogs which, with their owners, visit hospitals, nursing homes, and hospices, brightening the lives of people who may no longer be able to keep a dog of their own. Indeed it has been proved that the mere act of stroking a dog can help to reduce a patient's blood pressure.

The presence of dogs is being increasingly recognized as therapy and canines are finding their way, as residents, into a growing number of psychiatric and geriatric hospitals and hospices.

In the United Kingdom it is not permitted to allow a dog to pull a cart on a public highway. But in America it is not unusual for a large dog to bring home the groceries in this fashion, while in Switzerland the Bernese Mountain Dog may be seen drawing a milk churn. In its native Germany, the Rottweiler was traditionally the butcher's dog.

Dogs do of course appear in films, television commercials, and on the live stage. But perhaps their most important task of all is as companion to the lonely and the elderly, those people who would have nobody to relate to were it not for their faithful friend, the dog.

Above: Dogs are always needed to join the Pro-Dogs Active Therapy team, but first they must pass a rigorous temperament test. Some top show dogs are on the register, as are crossbreeds and mongrels.

Below left: In 1916, a doctor in charge of a clinic for the war wounded in Germany was walking a blind man in the grounds when he was called away. He left his German Shepherd Dog in charge of the patient and, on his return, was so impressed with the way the dog had behaved that he vowed to begin training dogs as guides for the blind.

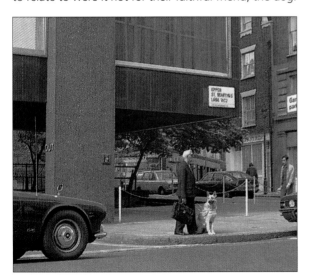

DR. DOG

One of the proudest chapters in sled dog history was written in 1925. It was in January of that year that a case of diptheria was discovered in Nome, Alaska. The supply of antitoxin in that city was insufficient to ward off an epidemic. A relay of 22 native and mail teams forged through the rough interior of Alaska and across the Bering Sea ice to bring the serum to the grateful citizens. Today in Central Park, New York, stands a statue of Balto, who led one of the relay teams, commemorating the Nome Serum Run. An inscription reads: "Dedicated to the indomitable spirit of the sled dogs that relayed antitoxin 600 miles over rough ice, treacherous waters, through arctic blizzards from Nemana to the relief of stricken Nome in the winter of 1925. Endurance, Fidelity, Intelligence."

Can Dogs Love?

The proverb says, "A dog never bites the hand that feeds it", and cynics may say that as dogs rely on us for their creature comfort, any show of affection is self-motivated—it wishes to safeguard its meal ticket. There have, however, been far too many true stories illustrating the unselfish love of dogs for their masters for such arguments to carry much weight.

It must be admitted that dogs thrive best, and are happiest, when their routine is undisturbed. Like humans, they become attuned to sleeping on a familiar bed, or basket; eating their dinner and going out for walks at regular hours. A break in routine when, for example, the family member who usually exercises the dog goes away, or it is put into boarding kennels, can account for loss of condition.

But there is no doubt that dogs, particularly those that live in close proximity to their owners, often sharing the same sleeping quarters, and rarely leaving their side, can literally pine to death should their owner predecease them.

THE STORY OF GREYFRIARS BOBBY

In my view, it is the true story of Greyfriars Bobby which best illustrates the lasting love of a dog for its master. Bobby was a small, shaggy terrier, possibly a Skye Terrier, the much-loved companion of a Midlothian farmer named Gray.

Each Wednesday, Bobby would accompany his master to market in Edinburgh and, at midday or thereafter, the two would repair to Traill's Tearooms where Gray had his midday meal and Bobby would be given a bun. In 1858, Gray died, and was laid to rest in Greyfriars Churchyard.

On the third day following the funeral, at the usual time of Gray's visit, Bobby, bedraggled and looking the picture of woe, presented himself at the tearooms where, out of pity, Traill gave the dog its customary bun.

It was thought that this would be the last that those at the tearooms would see of Bobby. But the next day and the day after, the dog appeared and again was given, and trotted off with, its bun.

Finally, his curiosity aroused, Traill decided to follow Bobby. This he did, and was surprised to find the little dog heading for Greyfriars Churchyard. When the dog got there it lay down on its master's grave and ate its scanty lunch.

It soon became evident that Gray had been a loner and that no provision had been made for Bobby; also that the little dog was spending its days and nights lying on the grave, leaving its vigil only to go to the tearooms when forced to do so by pangs of hunger.

TREKKER SETTER

Some dogs love their home almost as much as their master. In August 1976 an Irish (Red) Setter named Bede went missing while on holiday in Cornwall with his owner, Father Louis Heston. Almost six months later, Bede, footsore and weary, turned up at his master's home in Braintree, Essex, having travelled 300 miles (480km). The Kennel Club declared Bede the Bravest Dog of 1976 and he was presented with his award at Crufts dog show on 12 February 1977.

Below: Dogs enjoy human companionship. They like to be close to their owners, and often enjoy accompanying them during routine daily activities.

DOG POWER

In some parts of the United States, canine weight-hauling contests are very popular—competing dogs testing their strength and endurance by pulling heavy loads. The World Championship Weight Hauling Contest is held at Bothell, Washington, as part of the annual Northwest Newfoundland Club Working Dog Trials. There are five weight categories: under l00lb (45kg), l00–130lb (45–59kg), 130–165lb (59–75kg), 165–190lb (75–86kg) and over 190lb (86kg). However, the greatest recorded load to have been shifted by a dog was 6,400.5lb (2905kg) pulled by a 176lb (80kg) St. Bernard named Ryettes Brandy Bear at Bothell on 21 July 1978, on which occasion the other dogs entered, three Newfoundlands, two Alaskan Malamutes, and another St. Bernard, also pulled 25 times their own bodyweight on their first haul.

Above: Play is a good way to build up friendship and loyalty between owner and dog, as well as reinforcing training lessons.

Normally, dogs were not allowed into Greyfriars Churchyard, but the rule was eventually waived in the case of Bobby who, taking refuge only in wet weather in a nearby shelter provided by compassionate friends, and refusing any attempt at rehoming, continued his vigil for the next 14 years until his death in 1872, when he was buried, like his master, in Greyfriars Churchyard.

Later, a statue of Bobby was erected by the people of Edinburgh to commemorate this little dog who, even following his master's death, could not be persuaded to leave his side.

Below: Most dogs are keen to please their owners, and once trained they can be encouraged to carry out all kinds of tasks and activities.

Where Can I Get a Dog?

Once you have decided whether you want a purebred, crossbred, or mongrel, you must make up your mind if you would like a dog or a bitch. This is entirely a personal choice. Many people prefer bitches, believing them to be easier to train, and because of their gentler, maternal nature, a better companion for children. Others welcome a dog's more zestful approach to life. However, it is worth mentioning that the woman who buys a bitch may find that it becomes more attached to her partner while the dog, intended as the man's companion, prefers the lady.

CHOOSING A DOG

Also to be considered is whether the dog is to be big or small, and short- or long-coated, bearing in mind that the long coat will require extensive grooming and that even a short-coated breed with a light coat will deposit noticeable hairs on the carpet.

Mongrels and crossbreeds can be obtained from pet stores, from the rescue kennels of animal welfare societies, and through advertisements in local newspapers. You may even see pups advertised on postcards in store windows. If you have not set your heart on a puppy, you could be doing a misplaced, older dog a favor by offering it a home. There are likely to be several to choose from at your local breed rescue kennels.

If you want a purebred, much depends on whether you are looking for a pet or show dog, because the

SAFETY NET

● Breed rescue societies have been set up by almost all breed societies in an effort to rehome misplaced members of their breed—dogs of various ages whose owners have had to relinquish them for a variety of reasons.

● Breed rescue offers an opportunity for those seeking a particular breed, but reluctant or unable to take on a puppy, to obtain an older dog of their favorite breed. Obviously only genuine applications are considered and "rescue" should not be regarded as a cheap means of obtaining a purebred dog.

purebred dogs you see advertised in newspapers, or glimpse in pet store windows, are unlikely to be destined for the show ring.

Once you have narrowed down your choice to one or two breeds, a call to your national kennel club will elicit details of reputable breeders. Bear in mind that, if you live in a city, it is unlikely that a breeder of, say, Mastiffs will live around the corner, so you must be prepared to travel some distance, and to have your name put on a waiting list.

Don't be put off if breeders ask lots of questions—whether you have a garden, for instance, and whether you have a job, or are at home all day. The mere fact

Character is formed early. Always choose an inquisitive, confident pup. A timid one is likely to grow into a nervous dog.

Above: You should make sure that the puppy of your choice is healthy before finalizing the purchase. **1.** Pick up the puppy to check that it does not object or show signs of pain; its body should be firm and relaxed. **2.** Lift the ear flap and check that the ear canal is dry and clean. **3.** Open the mouth gently and check that the tongue and gums are pink. **4.** The eyes should be clear and bright, and there should be no signs of discharge. **5.** Run your hand against the grain of the coat to check for sores and the black dust caused by fleas. **6.** Check under the tail that there is no staining, which would indicate diarrhea.

of their doing so proves that they have the welfare of their stock at heart. If you would like a purebred that is well past puppy stage, even five years of age or more, ask your national kennel club to let you have the address of the relevant breed rescue society. They might have a dog of the chosen breed needing rehoming for any number of reasons, ranging from the death of a previous owner to a marriage breakup.

Don't make a hasty decision about your choice of dog. After all, it is destined to be your companion for twelve years or maybe more.

DO'S AND DON'TS

Do check that everyone in your home really wants a dog.

Do be prepared to travel some distance. It is usually only breeders of toy varieties that can be found in big cities.

Do ask to see the dam of the litter. This will give you an idea what your pup will look like when full grown.

Do make sure that the Certificate of Pedigree is in order and that this, and the transfer form, have been signed by the breeder.

Don't buy a dog if you are out at work all day.

Don't choose a long-coated breed if you haven't the time to groom it.

Don't buy an Afghan Hound when you really set out to buy a Yorkshire Terrier.

Don't buy a "pet" quality dog if you plan to exhibit it in purebred classes.

Above: The Wood Green Animal Shelter in England is one of the most modern in Europe. Records of every inmate are held on computer.

Getting Ready for Your New Pet

There are items to be bought, and precautions to be taken, before your pup arrives.

First of all, make sure that your yard is adequately fenced. If it is not, arrange for the work to be carried out speedily, bearing in mind that gates and fencing must be flush with the ground, and that the foot of the netting must be buried to ensure that tiny breeds cannot crawl underneath.

Experienced dog owners lucky enough to have big yards often net or fence off an area especially for their pets. This enables them, particularly if they are keen gardeners, to safeguard the remaining area for horticulture. However, you may wish to confine your dog to a paved yard, which can be easily swilled down with a disinfectant solution. There are disposal units for canine excrement available from pet stores and hardware suppliers.

WHAT TO BUY

An indoor wire pen, with a plastic, removable floor tray, is an excellent investment, and can be obtained in various sizes. Into the pen will go the pup's basket, preferably of the polyurethane type (wicker would be

LEASH: YES—HARNESS: NO

Some pups take longer than others to react favorably to a leash. Although it is tempting to resort to a harness, which has the effect of lifting the pup bodily, rather than pulling from the neck, it is not recommended as it will spoil your pet's future walking action.

chewed to pieces), his synthetic wool bedding, and toys; the remainder of the base being covered with newspaper and housing a water bowl. The pup can sleep in the pen and be placed in it whenever you need to slip out for a few hours, thus alleviating any problem of chewed slippers—or furniture! The pen should be placed in a warm, draft-free position.

Also needed would be a feed bowl, soft puppy brush, and a puppy leash and collar. But please don't invest in a harness. It is admittedly easier to teach a pup to accept a leash with this item of equipment, but you risk spoiling its movement.

Plastic bed

Plastic bed

Vet bed

Padded bed

China bowl

Metal bowl

Plastic bowl

Rubber "tug"

Rubber ball
and ring

Leather collar
and leash

Puppy collar
and leash

Nylon collar
and leash

Identity tag

Check chain

Above: The caged pet will not chew furniture and rarely soils its bed. Indoor kennels are a boon for house training and for times when you want to leave your pet for short periods, but don't keep it shut up too long!

Left: There are numerous types of beds and bedding and other canine equipment available. It is a good idea to visit a dog show, where there will be numerous trade stands. You can then view a wide range of equipment, and discuss your needs with professionals. Remember that a pup will soon outgrow its collar, and will chew a basket, so it is best not to invest too much money until it has matured.

Check with the seller as to the pup's customary food—a breeder will give you a diet sheet. Even if you have other feeding plans, it is best not to alter the pup's dietary routine for the first few days.

Finally, do make sure that toys are of hard, durable plastic that cannot be swallowed; those of the old-fashioned rubber type are ideal. If your dog is destined to be a lightweight, think in terms of a carry box which will be a boon for transporting it to shows, to the veterinarian's office, on vacation, or simply for trips in the car. As a temporary measure, a cardboard carry box can usually be obtained from animal welfare societies.

KENNEL COMFORTS

Most pet dogs live in the house with their owners. Toy and short-coated breeds almost always do so. However, owners of working and gundog breeds often prefer to kennel them out of doors. This does not involve less work. Kenneled dogs have to be fed, watered, groomed, exercised—and indeed cleaned out—just like their indoor counterparts. Heating should be provided in cold weather; heat lamps and space heaters are two of the systems widely used.

Giving Your Dog a Proper Diet

Basically, dogs have the same nutritional requirements as ourselves. They need a balanced diet containing protein (meat), carbohydrates (cereals), and fat, with minerals and vitamins added. Almost all types of meat are suitable excepting liver, which is a laxative and should be fed only in strict moderation.

Water is essential and must be supplied either (almost always) as drinking water, or in the food itself. Ground meat contains about 70 percent water.

FRESH MEAT VERSUS BRANDED PET FOOD

It does not seem so long ago that conscientious dog owners insisted on feeding pets fresh meat, using prepared dog foods only as a standby. And indeed a diet of water, and suitable meat and biscuits do meet the basic food requirements of the dog in full.

Nowadays however, branded pet foods have been scientifically prepared to meet the nutritional requirements of the dog and are fed by most kennels and individual dog owners, as much for the benefit of the dog as for convenience. These prepared foods come in the form of meaty canned products, to which dog biscuits should be added, cans of complete, or soft, moist foods that do not require the addition of biscuits, or a complete dry dog food to which only water is added. The dry foods do increase a dog's thirst, so if they are used, it is necessary to ensure that the drinking water supply is well topped up.

Below: Dogs guard their food jealously. However, aggressive behavior toward humans over the dinner bowl should not be tolerated.

And, while many dog owners still insist on feeding pups on lightly cooked, lean ground beef for the first few weeks from weaning, canned puppy food is available, which has been specially formulated with all the nutritional requirements needed to give pups a good start in life.

Puppy feeding schedule		
Age	**Feeds per day**	**Approx. time of feeds**
From weaning to 3 months	4	Breakfast, lunch, supper
3–6 months	3	Breakfast, supper
6–12 months	2	Breakfast (or early supper)
One year and over (The dog is an adult at one year)	1 or 2	Lunchtime and/or early evening (If lunchtime, a few biscuits should be given at bedtime.)

Note: The exact time of feeds is flexible, but once chosen they must be strictly adhered to. Initially the pup should receive two milky meals (a prepared baby food is ideal) and two meals of lightly cooked, lean, ground beef or canned puppy food.

Feeding the adult dog		
Quantities based on average 13½oz (380g) can:		
Toy-sized dog	e.g. Yorkshire terrier	¼–½ can
Small-sized dog	e.g. West Highland White terrier	½ can
Medium-sized dog	e.g. Cocker spaniel	1 can
Large-sized dog	e.g. Labrador retriever	1½–2 cans
Very large sized dog	e.g. Great Dane	4 cans

It will be appreciated that some dogs burn up more energy and have a greater need for food than others, so once you have ascertained the correct weight for your dog you can adjust its rations accordingly. Consult your veterinarian if in doubt.

MEALTIME TIPS

● If you feed a dog late at night you only have yourself to blame if it is not clean in the morning.

● It does not matter whether you feed your adult dog once or twice a day dividing the food ration into two portions. However, toy breeds with small stomachs often fare better on two or even three little meals a day.

● On average a dog weighing 10lb (4.5kg) needs 8oz (225g) of food a day. A dog weighing about 25lb (11kg) needs 1¼lb (565g).

● Never, ever, give your dog poultry bones. They could be swallowed whole and splinter inside its stomach.

Dog food comes in a variety of forms. In the beginning you will need to try out different types of food to see which suits your dog best.

Semi-moist meat

Canned meat

Complete dried food

Fresh meat

Dog biscuits

Chew sticks

Vitamin treats

Rawhide chew

Puppy mixer meal

House-Training

It is unlikely that a pup will come to you ready house-trained, if for no other reason than that breeders, perhaps with several litters to look after, simply do not have the time to do it.

Some pups are house-trained within a matter of weeks. Others take considerably longer. It is something that is achieved by diligence and patience, not by bullying or adopting the unpleasant habit of rubbing the pet's nose in the offending spot.

Most likely the pup has been conditioned to answering the call of nature on newspaper, and further paper training is recommended.

Once your pup has grown up it will be able to control its bladder for a matter of hours. In puppyhood it cannot do so, and you must be prepared for mistakes.

DO'S AND DON'TS

Spread newspaper fairly liberally on the kitchen floor and, whenever you see the pup about to squat, lift it up firmly but kindly, point to the paper and place it on it. Do this even if it has erred, but NEVER hit it if it has not used the newspaper.

Once the pup shows signs of understanding what is required, continue the practice, but substitute the

SOME BASIC RULES

● If you are out at work all day, it is unfair to keep a dog no matter how much you may love them, unless, of course, you have a friend or helper who could be relied upon to call at your home every mid-day to exercise the pet in your absence.
● Never, ever hit a dog. Your tone of voice should be sufficient to express displeasure and a dog wants only to please. Be generous with praise whenever a dog does well, patting it, and saying "Good boy" or "Good girl" as the case may be.

generously spread paper with just a sheet or two at the back door. Once pup knows to toddle to the door when it wants to relieve itself you can start opening it and letting it out into the garden, praising it lavishly when it does what is required. But don't, please, leave it out in the cold for an inordinate length of time. Some dogs, like some people, take a little longer to understand what is required of them than others.

1 When your pup relieves itself, place it promptly on the sheets of newspaper that you will have placed on the kitchen floor.

2 Soon the pup will look for the newspaper when it needs to answer the call of nature and will toddle onto it, but be prepared for the occasional mistake.

Obviously one does not want an adult dog to relieve itself in the house as a matter of course. However, the mere fact of having been paper trained in puppyhood can be enormously beneficial in the case of tiny breeds if, for example, you are going out and know that your return may be delayed. In such a case, simply leave a sheet of newspaper by the door. The dog will know what it is there for.

HOW LONG TO LEAVE YOUR DOG?

New owners often ask how long they may leave their pet before returning to let it out into the garden. Bearing in mind that it is always best to leave a young dog only for short periods until it has had time to build up confidence in your return, it should, in adult life, be capable of being left for about five hours. There are, in most people's lives, the odd occasions that compel them to extend this period. However, the truth of the matter is that the person whose job demands their being out of the house from nine to five should not consider dog ownership. The dirty, noisy, and destructive dog is usually also a lonely one.

Below: When you are fairly confident that the pup has performed, open the door, let the pup in, and praise it lavishly. It is always much easier to house-train a pup when it has an older canine companion to show it the ropes.

3 Gradually decrease the amount of newspaper and leave a sheet or two by the back door.

4 Soon, if the weather is warm, you can open the back door when the pup heads toward it, and encourage it to go outside.

Training Your Dog

Your pup should not be taken for a walk until it has had its full quota of inoculations. This presents you with an ideal opportunity to prepare it for the adventure, by accustoming it to a leash and collar.

ATTACHING A COLLAR

First of all, let it get used to wearing a collar for short periods, making sure that it is not too tight. You should be able to place two fingers' width underneath, without fear of it pulling over its head.

Now attach the leash and, after the pup has played with it for a little while, pick it up and place it at arm's length in front of you.

Next, holding the lead in your right hand, and offering a tidbit with your left, pull the leash gently toward you. Once the pup gets the idea, start walking slowly backward, gradually increasing the distance.

Once this exercise has been accomplished and the pup is no longer fighting the restriction of the leash and collar, you can begin leading it on your left hand side, reducing the number of tidbits, but praising the pup's progress lavishly. But a word of warning: do not let this, or any other lesson, continue for too long, and always end on a note of encouragement.

GOING FOR "WALKIES"

Once the pup is bigger, and you venture out with it onto the road, it should walk on your left you should hold the loop of the leash in your right hand, and hold

REMEMBER...

● Dog training exercises should initially be taught with the dog's leash and collar on.
● A choke chain should not be used on a toy breed. These are frequently used in training large breeds, but increasingly they are being replaced with those of strong nylon, particularly where the practice of leading the dog from the head, rather than the neck, is adopted.
● Your dog's collar should be removed when it is at rest, and particularly before it goes to sleep at night. Not only is this more pleasant for the dog, but it prevents the collar marking its coat.

the part about halfway up from the clip with your left, so that the leash extends across your body, and you are able to exert good control.

TEACHING "SIT" AND "STAY" COMMANDS

Regardless of whether you want your dog to be simply a household pet or to compete in obedience or conformation classes, it is necessary to teach it to "sit," "stay," and "come" when called. By teaching it the "stay" command you could, for instance, prevent it from rushing across a road and having an accident or indeed causing one.

Left: Training classes are an excellent place to teach your dog obedience, as you can work under the eye of a professional.

1 When leash training, have the dog walking on your left. Hold the end of the leash in your right hand, and take up most of the slack in your left hand. Give the command you are going to use, such as "heel," and walk off. Every time the dog pulls away, give a small jerk on the lead with your left hand, but release it again as soon as the dog returns to the correct position.

2 There are several ways in which to teach a dog to "sit." Here is one of the easiest: with the dog walking on your left, hold the leash up with your right hand and, with your left, firmly press the dog's hindquarters down, at the same time firmly uttering the command "sit." Keep doing this during your walk until it gets the idea of what is required.

3 The "stay" command is a progression from "sit." Put your dog in the "sit" position. Now move in front of the dog saying "sit," then "stay" very firmly, jerking on the leash if it attempts to move. If it does so, you must start again.

4 & 5 Tremendous patience is called for in dog training. Once the dog knows how to "sit" and "stay" you can begin using the command "stay" as you gradually move farther away from it.

6 The "come" (or recall) command is an advanced progression of the puppy leash training when you drew the bewildered pup toward you. Now you can adopt the same procedure uttering the command "come" once your pet is in the "sit–stay" position, and making a great fuss of it when it obeys, so that it associates the command with a pleasing experience.

Can I Learn How to Show My Dog?

Don't try to run before you can walk is good advice. Yes, there are those who enter a championship show with an untried dog and win their class, but this doesn't happen very often.

It is sensible to enrol your pup in a handling class. In any case, you will not be permitted to exhibit it in Kennel Club-recognized shows until it is six months of age.

The handling class (not to be confused with the dog training class, where your dog would learn obedience) is of help in accustoming the dog to mix with its own kind—and with people. You, in turn, will learn how to present your dog in the ring, using the correct technique for the breed.

For example, while one would walk in the ring with a French Bulldog or a toy breed, such as a Brussels Griffon or Chihuahua, it is necessary to run (gait) large breeds such as the elegant Afghan Hound or Doberman.

While toy dogs are examined by the judge on a table, except for the perky Yorkshire Terrier, which is examined on its own show box, large breeds are examined on the ground, standing in show stance.

GETTING YOUR EYE IN

It is sound advice, before commencing your showing career, to attend as many dog shows as you can, and to watch handlers of your particular breed. Study how their dogs stand and move and try to emulate this in your practice sessions.

Above: Toy dogs are examined standing on a show table. Most aspirants practice standing their pet on the table for a few minutes each day from a very early age. This is something that can be done during the daily grooming session.

In the United Kingdom there are many exemption dog shows, the word "exemption" meaning that they are exempt from most Kennel Club rules. These shows are an excellent platform for the beginner and include fun classes, such as "the dog with the waggiest tail," "the dog in best condition,"—and so on, and others for dogs that are not of pure breeding.

The exemption show is unlike the sanction show, which is open to members of the organizing club only, while open shows and championship shows are for the seasoned exhibitor. It is at the latter that Challenge Certificates are on offer, whereby one's dog or bitch may be chosen as the best example of its breed. Three Challenge Certificates awarded by three different judges at three different championship shows entitles the dog to be known as a champion.

Left: Handling classes provide an excellent opportunity for a young dog to become accustomed to walking with its fellows and being examined by a stranger. The handler learns what to expect in the show ring and the various procedures involved. Classes are usually held on a weekday evening.

In the United States, dog matches are a good training ground. They produce awards, but not the necessary points toward championship status, which can only be achieved at dog shows.

Points toward a Championship are won at specialty and all-breed shows, in five regular classes known as Novice, Bred by Exhibitor, American Bred, Open, and Puppy (6–9 and 9–12 months). The winners of such classes subsequently have to compete against each other to select a winning dog. The same system then follows for finals to select a winning bitch.

Judging systems vary from country to country but basically a winning dog in one country should be a winning dog in another. The judges are always looking for the dog which most exactly fits the standard for its breed.

Right: A rosette such as this could be the reward for a best in breed win at a dog show.

Left: A successful exhibitor demonstrates how to present a Hungarian Vizsla in the show ring. Showing a dog is not as easy as it looks. It is important to select a breed in keeping with your own physical capabilities.

DO'S AND DON'TS

Do dress smartly in the show ring so as to complement your dog.

Do wear sensible shoes. Some shows are held in a muddy field—no place for perilously high heels.

Do invest in a ring clip, so that the judge and steward can easily detect the number on your card.

Do study the catalog carefully and make sure that you are at the ringside in time for your class.

Do make sure that you take a bowl and water supply to the show for your dog.

Don't chat with other exhibitors in the ring.

Don't question the judge's decision.

Don't get cross with your dog if it does not perform as it might. Every dog has its day!

Grooming Your Dog

Whether pet or show dog, your canine companion will benefit from daily grooming. This daily beauty treatment not only makes your pet look and feel good, but gives the owner an opportunity to check for possible flea infestation or any minor injuries or other problems.

Of course, some breeds need considerably more grooming than others, so if your time is strictly limited it is advisable not to choose a breed that requires intricate preparation, especially if it is destined for a show career.

Most short-coated breeds are fairly easy to look after. All they need is grooming with a brush of short, stiff bristles, or with a hound glove. A rub-down with a velvet pad also works wonders, and so does brisk toweling. For heavy-coated breeds you need a brush with nylon bristles.

CLIPPING, COMBING, AND PLUCKING

The show preparation of some breeds is by no means easy for the novice to undertake. The Poodle, for example, needs its coat clipping about every six weeks and, while the attractive lamb clip will suffice for a pet, an intricate lion cut is obligatory for show, and this can take many hours to perfect.

The glamorous Afghan Hound and popular Old English Sheepdog are but two breeds that require lengthy preparation, while terriers must be hand stripped; the Bichon Frisé clipped and elaborately scissored, and the Hungarian Puli has the thick cords of its coat separated by hand. Other breeds, such as the comical little Brussels Griffon, must be knowledgeably plucked.

Usually the relevant breed club can supply information and a pattern chart of what is required.

SHOWTIME TURNOUTS

- **Breeds that are fairly simple to prepare for the show ring:** Boxer, Dachshund (smooth coat), Doberman, English Bull Terrier, French Bulldog, Smooth-coat Chihuahua, Griffon (Petit Brabançon), Pug, Staffordshire Bull Terrier.
- **Breeds that require maximum preparation:** Afghan Hound, Airedale Terrier, Wire-haired Fox Terrier, Bichon Frisé, Komondor, Lhasa Apso, Poodle, Portuguese Water Dog, Pekingese, Old English Sheepdog, Puli, Shih Tzu, Yorkshire Terrier.

soft brush

rubber brush

hound glove

chamois sponge
wire comb

plastic comb

wire brush

ear wipes and
eye wipes

nail clippers

toothbrush and
paste

Left: It is sensible, when you buy a pup, to discuss with the breeder the basic equipment you will need. Later, if you decide to show the pup, you could require such items as portable trolleys for benching pens, grooming tables and show leads.

CROPPING AND DOCKING

Many working breeds (such as the Boxer, Great Dane, and Doberman), utility breeds (such as the Schnauzer) and toys (such as the Miniature Pinscher and Brussels Griffon) have their ears cropped in their country of origin. However, the practice is illegal in the United Kingdom, Scandinavia, Australia and, depending on individual State law, in the USA. Tail docking has also been banned in Sweden, and controversy rages as to the rights and wrongs of this practice in other countries.

Canine beauty parlors will undertake the work for you, but most owners take pride in personally ensuring the immaculate turnout of their breed.

There are a number of routine jobs that must be done when you groom your dog. You must, for instance, remember to clean inside its ears with cotton wool moistened with olive oil, taking immense care not to probe too deeply; wipe away any stains around the eyes with cotton wool dipped in lukewarm water, or cold tea, and clean your dog's teeth with a proprietary brand of canine toothpaste.

It is not usually necessary to bath pet dogs except in summer time when, after brisk toweling, they can run about and get dry in the garden. However, show dogs are, in the main, bathed the night before, or a few days before a show, depending on the type of coat. This is a matter on which the breeder can best advise you.

CLIPPING AND CURLING

• Some people buy a long-coated breed because they love grooming. They may sit, with their dog on their knees, all evening, meticulously working on its coat. If, unlike them, your time is limited, it is better to choose a short-coated breed.

• Dogs that receive regular pavement walks usually wear down their nails as a matter of course. Most breeds,

however, need to have theirs clipped with veterinary clippers every few months. Take care not to clip beyond the quick (the white part of the nail) or bleeding and pain will be caused. Don't be afraid to ask the breeder, or your veterinary surgeon, to show you how to tackle this task.

• The perky little Yorkshire Terrier that you may see running around, covered in mud, is very different from its sedate, exhibition cousin, which spends most of its time wearing paper curlers.

Ears: Check the ears and earflaps for any sign of wax or an unpleasant smell, which could be signs of canker. Ear wipes are available, but never probe the ear.

Nails: If your dog gets plenty of roadwork, its nails should wear down naturally. If not, they will need to be trimmed with veterinary clippers about every three months. The veterinarian will undertake this task.

Eyes: Check the eyes for any inflammation and watering; also for opacity in the cornea. For routine care it is possible to buy eye wipes specially formulated to clean the discharge often found around the eye area.

Teeth: It is sensible to take your dog to the veterinarian for regular scaling. This is particularly important in the case of toy breeds, which can lose their teeth at an early age.

Exercising Your Dog

All dogs need exercise. There are breeds that can manage with very little exercise and others that need a great deal, so it would be unwise to buy a breed with limited walking capacity if you are an ardent rambler, or a large working breed if you are somewhat lethargic.

Most dogs need, on average, two good twenty-minute walks a day, preferably with some off-the-leash gambols in a suitable recreation area. If you have a fairly large yard, the latter is not so important, and you can play ball with your dog!

Working breeds, in particular, need plenty of exercise. If you can channel their energy and intelligence into a task such as obedience trials or agility, so much the better. You can start them off by enrolling at your nearest dog training club.

Below: A dog looks forward to its walk and will be disappointed if it does not occur at the usual hour. Often the owner would themselves not bother to exercise were it not for their canine companion.

OUT AND ABOUT

● Lap dogs such as the Pekingese, Yorkshire Terrier, and Pomeranian enjoy nothing better than going for walks across the fields and getting gloriously muddy, but, when occasion demands, a walk in the park, or a romp in the garden will suffice.

● Working breeds (e.g. the German Shepherd Dog, Doberman, Border Collie, Rottweiler, and Mastiff) can become restless and ill-natured if they do not have a task to perform. These dogs were bred to serve man, not to spend their days in an apartment block.

Toy dogs will keep happy and healthy with fairly limited exercise, but they enjoy a walk in the park and it would be wrong to deprive even a tiny Chihuahua of its daily outing. Some toy breeds will literally walk their owners off their feet!

The Bulldog is a breed that cannot walk very far, certainly for no more than half a mile (1km)—ideal for the retired elderly owner. It is vital that this breed is never taken out in very hot weather since, in common with other flat-nosed breeds which experience breathing difficulties, it might suffer. Sensible owners never travel with these breeds during a warm spell without wet towels and ice packs with which to revive them.

TAKING PUPPIES FOR WALKS

It is unwise to take a pup of any breed for long walks until it reaches six months of age, by which time it should have the necessary physique and stamina. Obviously you could not expect even a large, adult dog, which was out of condition, and had previously led a sedentary life, to go on a 10 mile (15km) walk. Distance must be worked up to gradually over a period of time. The Dalmatian, originally a carriage dog, is a breed that will tirelessly follow a horse, but so will many terrier breeds. I once met a miniature dachshund walking over the hills, far from home, with its master. It seemed a wonder that the dog had got so far on its very short legs but, as its master explained, the dog had been taken for long walks all its life and could therefore manage the distance.

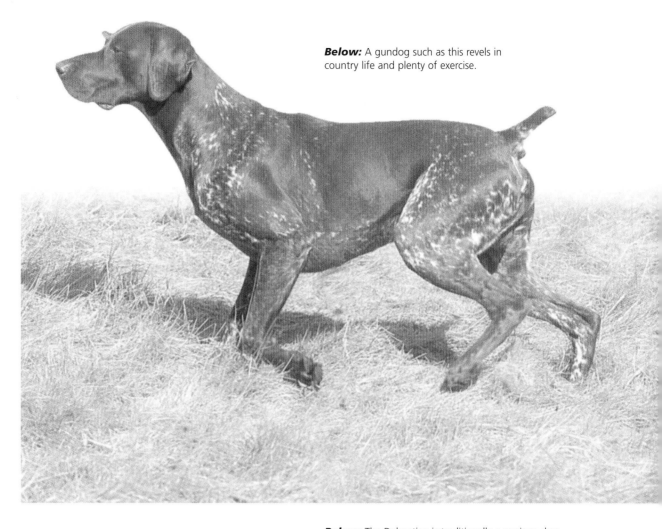

Below: A gundog such as this revels in country life and plenty of exercise.

Below: The Dalmatian is traditionally a carriage dog. However, it is not a good idea to exercise your dog from a bicycle or a slowly driven car as a substitute.

REGULAR ROUTINES

● Do try and establish a regular timetable for your dog's walks; for instance, early morning and afternoon, and perhaps a short stroll at bedtime. Remember that once the routine is set, your dog will be disappointed if, at the appointed hour, its walk does not materialize, just as it would be if, at dinner time, its dish were not to appear.

● The dog whose master took it for an afternoon walk when it was a puppy will remember and wait eagerly to go out—sometimes long after its insensitive master has forsaken the habit.

Should I Play With My Dog?

It is natural for dogs to play, and even the games played as puppies can be the prelude to a useful working role. The pup that runs and fetches a ball is learning a first lesson in how to retrieve. A game of hide and seek can be a preliminary to tracking.

Puppies enjoy playing together and, in the act of play-fighting, learn about dominance and submission. They learn that it is possible to play-fight without having recourse to aggression—and that a bite can hurt! They chase and pounce, learning the rudiments of hunting, and they indulge in harmless sex play.

MOLDING YOUR DOG'S CHARACTER

A pup that becomes the companion of a withdrawn, introverted person, who does not play with it, is likely to develop into a serious dog with little sense of fun, unlike the pet of an outgoing individual which will be

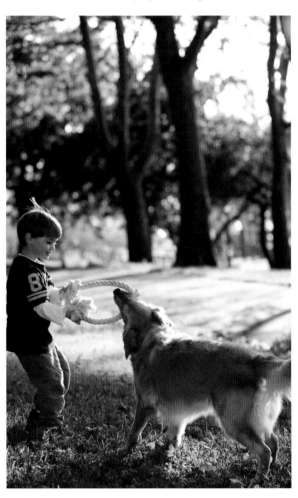

Below: Dogs are wonderful companions for children. Playing ball is fun for both child and dog. For the latter it can be a first step in learning how to retrieve. The young handler should be encouraged to take her pet to a dog training class where it will learn to socialize with other people and dogs.

eager and friendly like its master. There is a saying that "all work and no play makes Jack a dull boy." One could equally say that "all sleep and no play makes a dull dog."

Puppies are by nature lively, inquisitive, and playful. But in fact the character of a dog is formed by the time it is ready to leave the nest. The bold pup that comes forward to greet a visitor is destined to be an outgoing, fearless dog; the timid chap that slinks into a corner is likely to become a shy, nervous dog.

ORDER OF THE COLLAR

● Ever since ancient Egypt, paintings and sculptures have shown dogs wearing collars of various kinds. A wall painting in Pompeii shows a dog wearing a collar decorated with metal studs; a mosaic illustrates a chained dog wearing a plainer collar.

● The earliest collector of collars appears to have been Philip II of Spain who owned a collar that had belonged to the duke of Burgundy (1342–1404). It was described in the 1558 inventory of his possessions as being embroidered with pearls.

● Many collars from medieval times bore long, cruel-looking spikes, but these were intended to protect the dogs when they did battle with wolves and bears. Far more attractive to look upon is a large English brass collar from the late 18ᵗʰ century, inscribed: I am Mr. Pratt's Dog, King St. Nr. Wokingham, Berks. Whose dog are you?

Will My Dog Show Aggression?

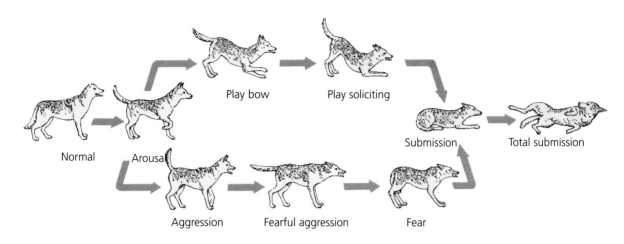

Play bow

Play soliciting

Submission

Total submission

Normal

Arousal

Aggression

Fearful aggression

Fear

The dog communicates through a variety of body positions and facial expressions.
The consecutive changes from normal stance to submission are shown here.

There are some breeds which were originally bred for their ferocity and guarding instincts others that were purely designed as gundogs, pets, and or for some other purpose. That is why it is so important to make the right choice for oneself.

Some breeds will accept other breeds into their social pack and are gregarious with other dogs that they meet. Some are not. It is, however, unusual for a puppy not to be accepted, though it should be introduced by easy stages, preferably on neutral ground.

It is a dog's instinct to guard its territory against all comers, hence the term watchdog, but while for example, an Irish Setter would probably welcome a burglar with a lick and a wag of its tail, a Bull Terrier having let him in might then stand guard while the quaking wrongdoer stands on a chair.

COMPARING TEMPERAMENTS

Accepting, then, that a Cavalier King Charles Spaniel differs in temperament from a Rottweiler, and that there is no inherited flaw, a dog that has been carefully selected from sound stock, brought into the home at an early age, and properly trained, should not show aggression.

It is however essential, particularly in regard to the larger, guarding breeds, that they do not get their way too much when they are pups lest they should, in frustration, turn on their owner when they are disciplined at a later stage, Most dogs, let it be said, just want to please.

Below right: Sometimes a court of law may order a dog to be destroyed or muzzled if it has a proven record of ferocity. In some countries an imported dog that has not been inoculated against rabies must be muzzled.

Left: This picture of a contest between animals c. 5th century BC comes from a Greek painted limestone relief at the National Museum in Athens. While man-and-dog fights were once common, the man sometimes having one arm tied behind his back, it is unusual to see two men with two dogs in a fighting pose.

Will My Dog Bark?

It is ironic that, while many people want a dog for its guarding abilities, which includes the ability to bark, nobody wants a yappy, noisy one that is likely to evoke complaints from neighbors.

It is normal for dogs to give warning when there is a knock on the door, or a noise in the night. Some even give a bark of delight in play. However, the incessant barker cannot be tolerated and could even result in legal action being taken against its owner.

THE YODELING DOG FROM THE CONGO

Some breeds are more noisy than others; toy dogs, for example, are notoriously yappy—if they are allowed to get away with it—as are some small terriers, while the French Bulldog is a relatively silent fellow and, likewise, the Basenji, the barkless dog from the Congo, which gives only a kind of yodel.

TEACHING DOGS TO SPEAK

Just as it is possible to teach a dog to "speak" with a bark when it is shown a treat, then by lifting a warning finger encourage it to speak "softer, softer" until a mere whisper allows it the prize, so it is possible to prevent a dog from yapping persistently in everyday life.

When the dog barks, walk into the room with a rolled up newspaper, bang it firmly on the table, and say "NO!" in your most disapproving tone, adding the

Below: Although a guard dog warns against intruders, a dog that barks persistently is a nuisance. Dogs must be taught at an early age to stop barking when ordered to.

Gently raising one's knee to a large dog's chest is a good way to prevent it from jumping up.

A rolled-up newspaper banged on the table with a vocal command, "no," should stop it barking.

Water squirted over the dog from a hosepipe may be effective. This measure is sometimes adopted to stop dogfights.

words, "bad boy" (or girl). The suddenness of the bang should stop the dog in its tracks and it will cease barking. A clap of the hands generally has the same result. Again, a disapproving tone is all-important. Dogs do not like being in disgrace. Some will even slink off and sulk when they have been told off.

ANTISOCIAL BEHAVIOR

As a dog owner you are under an obligation morally and, in some cases, legally, not to allow your pet to disturb or cause distress and inconvenience to others by, for instance, fouling public footpaths and verges or worse, your neighbor's gate or garden frontage, and you must remove offending excrement should mistakes occur.

AN UNWELCOME WELCOME

Some people are passionately fond of dogs; others actively dislike them and could even interpret a boisterous, playful gesture on the part of the dog, such as rushing excitedly to the door with its owner, or leaping up at a visitor, as an attack. In addition, no one wants a dog to jump up at them when it has muddy paws. Unless therefore, you are confident that a visitor has a strong liking for dogs or that your dog will not jump up unless invited to, it is always best to shut your dog in an indoor kennel, or at least in another room, out of sight, until the visitor departs. It is better to be safe rather than sorry.

DOS AND DON'TS

Do curb your dog. This means ensuring that it deposits excrement in the gutter, not on the sidewalk, and that you subsequently always remove it in a suitable receptacle.

Do take out third party insurance lest your dog should cause a road accident or, perhaps, jump up at someone in play, tearing their clothing, or causing other damage.

Do shut up your dog when visitors call, unless you are confident that they are dog lovers.

Don't allow your dog to bark, taking it for granted that the neighbors don't mind. They probably do!

Don't allow your dog to jump up at people. They may think that they are being attacked. Some people are very frightened of dogs!

Below: Members of the dog's family may enjoy an enthusiastic greeting, but it is unlikely to be appreciated by visitors. And a dog that jumps up when its paws are muddy is a nuisance to everyone. Puppies should be taught that this behavior is not always appreciated.

Left: A pooper scooper is the easiest way to clear up after your dog.

Dogs and Vacations

Owning a dog does not mean an end to holidays, but it does mean making arrangements for your pet every time you decide to take a break, or even stay away overnight on a business trip.

Of course, you may have a reliable dog-loving neighbor who knows your dog and will be willing to take it in for the necessary period. Or its breeder may be more than willing to board it for you.

CHOOSING A GOOD BOARDING KENNEL

More likely, you will have to think in terms of booking your dog into a boarding kennel. Your veterinarian should be able to recommend establishments in your area. Pet stores and other dog owners can also generally supply helpful information and, likewise, public libraries, the commercial section of telephone directories, and your breed club. Like popular hotels, good boarding kennels are booked up well in advance, so it is sensible to make your reservation as soon as you have made your own plans.

A reputable establishment will expect you to provide your dog's proof of inoculation against killer diseases such as canine distemper, leptospirosis, infectious hepatitis, and parvo virus. Many now also require a certificate of inoculation against kennel cough. But don't be offended. You would not wish your pet to pick up a serious illness while in their care. Also required will be the name, address, and telephone number of your veterinarian, your own contact number while you are away, and details of your pet's customary diet and of any special medication.

CHECK IT OUT

● Do make sure that your dog will have its own kennel, and that there are adequate heating arrangements, particularly if it is a short-coated breed.
● Do ask about exercising arrangements. It is preferable for each dog to have a separate exercise run, but in some cases a kennel maid will take a number of dogs for a walk together.
● There is usually a daily charge for dog boarding. Often this is based on the size of dog, (toy, small, medium, and large), but sometimes a standard charge is made irrespective of size.

Left: Some owners think it kinder to leave their dog with a friend but there is always the risk that it might escape, which it is unlikely to do in a secure, well-run kennel.

Below: Most exhibitors of toy breeds use travel cases or crates to transport them safely. Obviously the dog must be allowed out to relieve itself at regular intervals.

You should ask the proprietor to show you where your pet will sleep and enquire about exercise arrangements. Ideally dogs should have individual kennels and exercise runs, as well as some form of heating.

Ask about baskets, bedding, and toys. Some kennels encourage owners to bring their pet's belongings; others would rather not take on this responsibility.

If it is your intention to board your dog for a number of weeks it might be sensible to book him in for a weekend beforehand, just so that he gets to know the routine, and realizes that he has not been abandoned.

TRIPS AWAY

Of course many people do take their dogs on holiday with them (but not usually abroad). There are hotels, particularly in country locations, that will accept pets. Motoring and hotel guides generally indicate whether this facility is available. In any case it is just as well to check with the manager at the time of making your booking rather than to turn up at the door with a Great Dane.

Where dogs are accepted at hotels it is usual for them to be allowed to sleep in the owner's bedroom, but not to accompany them into public rooms or any place where food is being served.

Some caravan parks also welcome well behaved dogs, particularly if they are kept on a leash.

Above: There are many caravan and camping parks that will welcome a well-behaved dog. It is sensible to check first, even if the chosen site does admit dogs, because they may have exceeded their quota.

Inoculations and Health Care

Within living memory, the chances of rearing a healthy pup were slim because of the scourge of distemper. Nowadays, due to advances in veterinary science, the risks have been virtually eliminated. However, the prospect of a pup contracting canine distemper and several other killer diseases still exists and it would be sheer folly not to have your pup inoculated against them.

The age at which your veterinarian prefers to inoculate puppies may vary slightly. Generally, a first inoculation is given at about eight weeks, with a follow-up four weeks later. On no account should the pup be taken for walks, or allowed to mix with other dogs, until the second inoculation has had time to take effect.

Above: Until a puppy's inoculations have had time to take effect, it is sensible for the owner to remove and disinfect their shoes when entering the home to minimize the risk of infection. You can exercise the puppy in your yard.

WORMING WARNING

Toxocara canis is the common roundworm deposited by infected dogs. If the resultant larva travels through the human body—for instance, where a child has touched dog feces while playing in a sandpit, and subsequently puts its fingers into its mouth—the result can be extremely dangerous. Hence the dire need for pups, and all dogs, to be wormed regularly.

KEEPING INOCULATION RECORDS

It is customary, once a pup's inoculations have been carried out, for the veterinarian to provide the owner with a record card. Here the pup's name, breed, sex and age are recorded; also the type, and dose of vaccine given. A reminder may be sent in twelve months' time, inviting the owner to bring the pup into the surgery for a booster. In any case, proof of up-to-date inoculation will be necessary if you book your dog into boarding kennels.

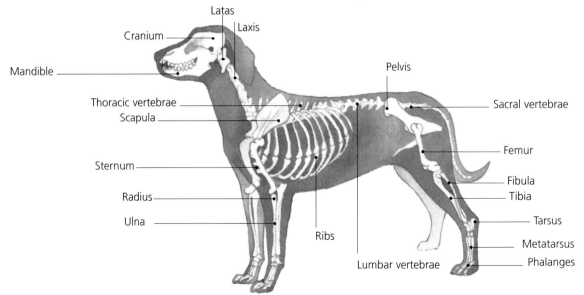

Latas
Laxis
Cranium
Mandible
Pelvis
Thoracic vertebrae
Scapula
Sacral vertebrae
Sternum
Femur
Radius
Fibula
Tibia
Ulna
Tarsus
Ribs
Metatarsus
Lumbar vertebrae
Phalanges

1 When giving a pill, make sure that it is slipped right down the throat. Often a dog will secrete the pill in its mouth and spit it out afterwards.
2 Stroke the dog's throat downwards to encourage it to swallow. Owners often disguise pills in a tidbit, such as a piece of cheese.

During the first few weeks after birth, pups are protected by antibodies received from their mother's milk—this is known as "maternally derived immunity." However, the protection wears off quickly and, thereafter, the pup may fall prey to all or any of the killer diseases, which is why vaccination is so important.
The inoculations that your veterinarian administers are likely to be those which provide protection against not only canine distemper, but also these:

• Canine parvo virus is a comparatively new disease first recorded in 1977. By the summer of 1978 it had become widespread, with large-scale outbreaks as far apart as Canada and Australia. It was first recorded in the United Kingdom in 1979.

FATAL FOR DOGS AND HUMANS

The killer disease Leptospirosis is caused by either of two microorganisms. The disease is spread by bacteria shed in urine—lampposts are a serious source of infection. One form of Leptospirosis is generally contracted from rats and, under the name Weil's Disease, can affect humans.

Parvo takes two forms—myocarditis, or inflammation of the heart muscle, in young pups up to eight weeks of age; and a severe gastro-enteritis, or inflammation of the stomach and intestines, from about five weeks through to adulthood. The death rate can be as high as 100 percent in young pups, but it reduces to around 10 percent in older pups and only about one percent in adult dogs.

Pups that survive myocarditis are frequently left with impaired heart function and may die prematurely, while survivors of the gastro-enteritis may remain in poor condition for a long period of time because of damage to the gut.

• Canine distemper is caused by a virus that can attack virtually all of a dog's body tissues.

• Viral hepatitis can cause damage to the liver, kidneys, and eyes. It may also be responsible for respiratory infection.

• Leptospirosis damages the kidneys and liver. You can see the extreme importance of not only having one's puppy inoculated but ensuring that booster inoculations are kept up-to-date.

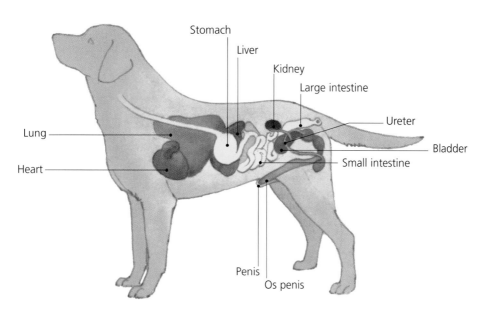

Canine Disorders

Ailment	Symptom	Action
Anal glands overfilled	Dog will rub hindquarters on the ground, showing obvious signs of irritation.	Dogs have little scent glands on each side of the anus. If they become overfilled they cause irritation and, if not relieved, abscesses may develop. The task of emptying the anal glands can be undertaken by the dog's owner once the veterinarian has demonstrated the correct procedure.
Bad breath	See Worms (could be stomach disorder)	Tablets available.
Broken leg		Call the veterinarian without delay. Do not give anything by mouth. Move the dog as little as possible and try to immobilize the broken limb by, for instance, tying it to its partner on the opposite side of the body.
Canker	Continuous shaking of head and rubbing against floor and furniture.	Canker is the name usually applied to all types of canine ear infection stemming from an accumulation of wax due to dirt or mites. It is sometimes detected by an accompanying unpleasant smell. There is any number of preparations available but first ascertain the cause of the trouble by consulting your veterinarian. Warm olive oil acts as a cleansing agent. It could well clear up the trouble.
Choking	Dog may try to vomit or tear at mouth with paw.	Endeavor to open dog's mouth and remove foreign body—a piece of bone or a chew could have become wedged across the roof of its mouth. In some cases, a general anesthetic may be needed, so check with your veterinarian.
Collapse	Dog will lie on its stomach and refuse to rise. May be breathing heavily.	Summon veterinary advice as soon as possible. Meanwhile, transfer patient onto a suitable mattress or blanket and keep warm. Bathe the mouth with glucose, or sugar in water. Do not force the dog to swallow. The dog should not be allowed to lie on one side for more than 20 minutes.
Cut foot	Sudden bleeding from foot, with or without lameness. This often occurs on beaches, and when dogs swim in ponds where there is broken glass. Similar symptoms may be shown when a claw is broken near its base.	If bleeding is profuse, wrap foot in lint or cotton wool and apply a firm roller bandage with even pressure a round the foot. Be careful not to bend a broken claw. Take the dog to a veterinarian for whatever treatment is necessary. Never use an elastic band or other constricting material.
Diabetes	Increased thirst and appetite, with associated weight loss.	Contact your veterinarian. You may have to learn how to give your dog daily injections of insulin.
Diarrhea (acute)	Very loose motions that may contain blood; can be accompanied by vomiting and weakness in the hind legs.	Starve the dog and keep it warm. Bathe the mouth and gums with a warm solution of glucose or sugar in water. Phone the veterinary surgery for advice.
Earache	The dog will scratch its ear, or ears, and may hold its head on one side and shake it.	There may be a grass seed in the ear. Contact your veterinarian. Meanwhile, do not put anything in the ear. It is easy for owners to make the wrong diagnosis, so it is best to wait for professional treatment.
Eczema	Can be wet or dry. An angry patch appears on the dog's coat causing it to bite and scratch it.	Causes range from diet deficiency to a hormone disorder. The veterinarian may try several treatments, from cream application to a course of injections, before the trouble is cleared up.
Fits	Sudden uncontrolled spasmodic movements, often with champing of the jaws, usually accompanied by salivation. The dog may fall onto its side. The muscles across the top of the head and down the neck may twitch violently.	Remove collar, if tight. Make sure that the dog cannot injure itself, for instance near a fireplace. Make sure that it can breathe by holding the head and neck, extended if necessary. Keep in a darkened, quiet room until you can get help, and prevent all sudden noises, doorbells, slamming doors, etc. Most fits are over quite quickly. Seek veterinary advice as soon as possible.
Fleas	Scratching. Poor coat condition.	There are four common types of external parasite: lice and their eggs (nits), which are found mainly in the dog's head; and fleas, ticks and mites, which may be found on its body. Treatment is available in the form of special shampoos, dusting powders, and aerosols. Fleas are brownish and easily detectable in a dog's coat. They leave their droppings, not their eggs, in the dog's coat.
Grass seeds	See Earache.	The seed may work its way into the ear canal, and should be removed by a veterinarian. Check that grass seeds—and items like chewing gum—do not become lodged in the paws.

Ailment	Symptom	Action
Heart attack	Usually self-evident. Often occurs in hot weather following exercise, particularly in the case of older—and flat-nosed—dogs.	Lay the dog on its right side with the head and neck extended. Open doors and windows to obtain as much fresh air as possible. If the tongue becomes blue, or breathing stops, massage the heart vigorously. Obtain veterinary help immediately.
Heatstroke	Panting and obvious distress.	Owners of flat-nosed breeds that are particularly susceptible to heatstroke should never travel without pre-soaked towels and a supply of icy water. The latter should be applied to the dog's head. WARNING: Never, ever, leave a dog in a car.
Incontinence	The dog's inability to refrain from relieving itself.	This is usually a sign of kidney failure as the dog approaches old age. The condition can be helped with medication.
Injured eye	One eye appears very sore, or is kept closed.	Look for, and carefully remove, any obvious foreign body, such as a grass seed. This may be done by washing the eye with clean, warm water and thus flushing out the foreign body. Keep the patient in semi-darkness. Take it to the veterinarian for treatment. If this is not possible immediately, put a drop of medicinal parafin or olive oil in the eye as an emergency measure and prevent the dog from rubbing the affected eye with its paws, or on the furnishings.
Kennel cough	Persistent cough, usually after a spell in boarding kennels.	Rarely serious. Prevention is better than cure as it is possible to vaccinate the dog by intranasal administration of a small dose of Intrac, using a specially designed applicator. Antibiotics should help existing sufferers.
Limp		This could be the result of something embedded in a paw, a cut, a torn muscle or ligament; or even in the case of an older animal, arthritis or rheumatism. Restrict the animal until the veterinarian has examined it.
Mange	Unsightly bare patches.	There are a number of varieties of mange: sarcoptic, demodectic, and otodectic, which affects the ears. It is caused by an infestation of mites, which burrow in the roots of a dog's coat. It is highly contagious and can be transferred not only from dog to dog, but also to humans. The necessity of washing one's hands thoroughly after applying ointment cannot be over-emphasized. The condition is curable, but it should be left to the veterinarian to recommend appropriate treatment.
Misalliance	Your bitch has accidentally been mated.	Your veterinarian can give an injection within 48 hours, but preferably within 24 hours, to prevent your bitch having puppies.
Poisoning	There may be sudden acute sickness, prostration or violent muscular movements.	There are many possible agents, including slug bait. If the dog is seen to swallow a known poison, induce vomiting by pushing a solution of salt (a teaspoonful in a tumbler of water for an average-sized dog) down the throat. Give milk if the substance swallowed is at all corrosive. Never do this more than once. Seek your veterinarian's advice quickly, taking with you the remainder of the poisonous agent, if known.
Road accident	You may witness the accident, or your dog may return injured or lame.	Restrain your dog if necessary to prevent further injury and get it and bystanders away from the road. Be careful with injured limbs. Put a cold compress using wet cotton wool or lint on any obvious bleeding points, but, above all, keep the dog warm and comfortable. Contact your veterinarian as quickly as possible. Don't leave your dog lying on the road.
Shock		Get the patient to a veterinarian as quickly as possible. Never give anything by mouth to an unconscious dog—it could choke and die.
Temperature		The best means of taking your dog's temperature is to insert the thermometer about 2in (5cm) into the rectum. The normal temperature is 101.5°F (38.9°C). A low temperature in dogs is serious—call the veterinarian.
Worms	Bad breath, poor coat, ravenous appetite, potbelly.	There are a number of types of worms: roundworms, tapeworms, hookworms, whipworms and, in some countries, heartworms. However, the most common is the roundworm (Toxocara canis), which is most prevalent in puppies and in bitches before and alter whelping. At such times worming is often recommended by veterinarians at two week intervals. Normally, however, worming is recommended every three to six months. Many veterinarians will offer a wormer whenever a dog is presented for a booster inoculation.

Should I Have My Dog Neutered?

A bitch comes into season twice a year, the first season, or heat, occurring when she is about six months of age. It lasts on average for three weeks.

During the season, the bitch is attractive to male dogs. However, she is generally ready to be mated between the tenth and the twelfth day, after she has shown color, although this can vary by a few days on either side. At this time the normally sedate bitch develops into a sex siren who will adopt every trick in the book to slip out and find a mate, irrespective of breed, while her owner may despair at the sight of canine suitors hanging about outside the house.

Responsible owners keep a watchful eye on their bitch during her season, keeping her strictly segregated from male admirers, except in the case of a planned mating. Many people do keep an unneutered bitch, but it is as well to be aware of the extreme vigilance necessary.

SPAYING BITCHES

Neutering of the female, known as spaying, is the canine equivalent of a hysterectomy. The bitch which has been spayed no longer comes into season, cannot have puppies, and will not have false pregnancies. It is a logical step if you do not wish to breed from your bitch and if she is particularly difficult to cope with when she is in season.

MILLIONS HOMELESS

It is estimated that as many as 10,000 cats and dogs are born every hour in the United States. The enormous scale of the problem is highlighted by the American Society for the Prevention of Cruelty to Animals (ASPCA): "Even if each family took in one of these animals, every American home would be filled within three years."

Also, unless your bitch is of particularly good stock and there is likely to be a demand for her progeny, it is worth remembering the very many unwanted puppies which are, alas, destined to join the large band of strays.

Spaying, however, is not a decision to be taken lightly and the operation, once carried out, is irreversible.

Neutering (castration) of the male dog is not carried out as frequently, but is sometimes recommended by veterinarians, particularly in the case of aggression, over-ardent dogs, and those that share their home with bitches.

Below: Spaying involves removing the reproductive organs of the bitch.

Below: Castration—removal of the testicles of the male dog—is not performed frequently. Some owners think it is an easy remedy when an adolescent dog shows early signs of sexuality.

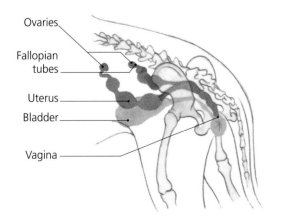

Ovaries
Fallopian tubes
Uterus
Bladder
Vagina

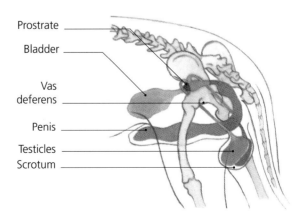

Prostrate
Bladder
Vas deferens
Penis
Testicles
Scrotum

What if I Want My Dog to Breed?

If you have dog breeding in mind with the sole aim of making easy money, the immediate advice is, forget it! Very few people make a living solely from dog breeding. Those who do are usually people who have had very many years' experience of exhibiting behind them. Now they probably specialize in a number of varieties, and often run boarding kennels as well.

For the most part, dog breeders are hobbyists; keen exhibitors intent on producing the ideal specimen of their breed, and with little financial reward in view other than recouping from their breeding activities the expenses they have incurred in veterinary fees, entry fees for shows, and traveling expenses, which are not inconsiderable when one realizes that championship shows may be held the length and breadth of the country. There are few weekends in the show season when keen exhibitors are not on the road in the early hours of the morning when most people are tucked in their beds.

If, however, you are determined to breed, it is advisable not only to have a few years showing experience first, but to invest thereafter in the very best bitch that you can afford. A "pet" quality bitch will produce only "pet" quality stock. You may say that you cannot afford the price, but it is far better to bide one's time and try to obtain a promising young bitch from a winning line, and subsequently mate her with a dog that has some form in the show ring. Possibly you may keep a bitch pup from her first or second litter, and gradually build up your breeding activities in that manner.

BREEDER'S TIPS

• Toy breeds generally have small litters of about four pups compared with large breeds, such as the Irish Setter and Golden Retriever, which can have seven pups or more. There are no hard and fast rules and it is believed by some that the day of mating can determine the number of pups in a litter.
• The novice breeder would be advised to steer clear of breeds with large heads (such as French Bulldogs, Pekingese, Boston Terriers) which are more prone than others to require cesarian delivery.
• Golden Retrievers, West Highland White Terriers, and Cavalier King Charles Spaniels are three breeds often chosen by the aspiring dog breeder.

Right: This family of Rhodesian Ridgebacks show the finest qualities of many European breeds blended with those of the Hottentot Hunting Dog. Note the distinctive ridge running from behind the shoulders to the haunches.

1 It is normal to take the bitch, when it is ready for mating, to the stud dog. If time permits, it is helpful if the pair have a chance to run together and become acquainted before the mating takes place.

2 Dogs will usually mate without human assistance, but not always. When assisting the mating of large breeds, a handler supports the bitch with his knee and also guides the dog, the bitch being firmly held by its owner. With toy breeds, a larger brood bitch is preferred. The dog is positioned on a block to give it the required height.

3 After a mating the dogs will tie. They will eventually break away naturally. The tie is not always necessary for a successful mating.

The Bitch In Whelp

It is not easy in the first few weeks following mating to determine whether your bitch is in whelp. Even a veterinarian would be unlikely to feel the tiny foetuses under four weeks.

However, at about the fifth week, prior to which the bitch may have carried the litter high in the ribcage, you will notice certain changes: her teats will start to develop and grow pink in color, and she may seem greedy for food and appear generally more maternal and loving.

At this stage, the bitch requires a third more food than usual. It should be mainly protein. Don't feed her up with starchy foods or these will result in her putting on too much weight.

Daily exercise should not be neglected until this causes discomfort. It is good for the bitch to keep her muscles active—also to be gently exercised following the birth to help regain her figure.

When the bitch reaches the seventh week of pregnancy, the litter will be carried downward, protruding low in the body. Now there may be less appetite because of the reduction of space in the abdomen. You can help by providing feed in the form of three or four small meals rather than one large one. Be prepared to bear with the bitch if she neglects her normally fastidious toilet habits. This also is because of pressure in the abdomen. She will be clean again after the birth.

Below: The Great Dane is a breed that needs warmth and, despite' its size, it is often whelped in a cozy corner of the kitchen. If you are considering keeping this variety, remember that it is expensive to feed.

THE WHELPING BOX

Remember that the pups will be coming into the world from a much warmer environment. Therefore, the whelping box, lined with newspaper, should be positioned where there is constant heat. It is important, particularly in the case of toy breeds, that the temperature at time of birth is about 80°F (27°C) and that this does not fall below 70°F (21°C) for the first three weeks of the puppies' lives.

CHECKLIST: WHAT WILL YOU NEED FOR THE MATERNITY WARD?

- Washable bedding, preferably of the synthetic sheepskin type
- Newspapers
- Roll of paper tissues
- Scissors
- Absorbent cotton
- Baby feeder—you may have to hand feed the puppies
- Towel
- Clock to time the intervals between births
- Pen
- Paper
- Your veterinarian's telephone number

The average time between the births of the first pup and the second range from 20–40 minutes, with an average 30 minutes between births. If the pups have not all appeared within three hours of the start of labor, or if the bitch is in distress, call your veterinarian immediately. You should have alerted him that the litter was due.

Weaning and Home-Finding

The bitch will feed her pups, and clean up after them for the first four weeks. However, at that time—sometimes before if she is not a very maternal bitch—she will want to revert to her normal way of life. She has done her job and now yours begins.

You can commence weaning by shutting the bitch away from the pups for a few hours a day until she is finally spending only the night with her litter.

The pups should be totally independent by the time they are six weeks of age, but this is rather young for them to go to new homes. Eight or preferably ten weeks is recommended.

Nowadays, with prepared puppy foods on the market, weaning puppies is considerably easier. However, any milky baby food, with glucose added, is an excellent starter to get pups lapping. Dip a finger in the saucer and allow them to lick. They will soon get the idea.

There are preparations formulated from skimmed milk to equate as near as possible to bitches' milk and this is also recommended. It is also beneficial for the bitch herself, prior to whelping.

Once the pups are taking their milk meals, you can introduce lean minced beef—raw, or preferably lightly cooked. Be sure that they are well weaned onto their

Below: Irish Setters often have large litters. Before the puppies go to their new owners, the breeder must make sure the pups can take milk and meat feeds.

The strongest pup will always try to take the lion's share. It is important to make sure that all the pups get their fill.

two milk meals and two meat meals a day before they go to new owners.

It is not as easy as you might think to find good homes for puppies. You can, of course, put an advertisement in your local newspapers and postcards in store windows. Much better, however, is to try and obtain bookings through the breed club or canine newspapers as soon as your bitch is in whelp, and to let your veterinarian know of the impending arrival. He may know someone who is looking for a pup—perhaps someone who has just lost an old canine companion.

Don't forget to give buyers a feeding chart along with the pedigree and transfer documents, and perhaps a little note asking the buyer to return the puppy to you if it does not suit. Better, surely, to have it returned to your care for rehoming than for it to end up, for some reason, in a pound. You should also let the buyer know the dates on which your puppies were wormed and hand over the vaccination record card if you have had the first inoculations administered.

Sometimes breeders take out an insurance against veterinary fees for the first few months of the pup's life; full details should be given to the buyer in case of a claim or if they should wish to renew the insurance cover when it expires.

WORMING WARNING

Pups should be wormed at five weeks and again at seven weeks. Adults should be wormed at six-monthly intervals.

How Long Will My Dog Live?

Dogs, like people, are, subject to illness and accident. Just as one member of a human family may outlive their brothers and sisters, so a litter member may have a longer, or shorter, lifespan than its fellows.

On average, a dog's lifespan is about twelve years. With advances in veterinary skills, many are living several years longer. There are however, breeds that are known for their longevity or otherwise.

The Great Dane, for instance, rarely goes beyond seven to nine years; likewise, the Bulldog. Poodles, Yorkshire Terriers, Chihuahuas, Schipperkes and small terriers, on the other hand, often live well into their teens.

You will also find that very often the dog whose parents and grandparents have lived to a great age is likely to do so too.

AN EYE FOR AN EYE

The longest serving guide dog in Britain is reckoned to have been Emma, a black Labrador Retriever that belonged to Sheila Hocken of Stapleford, Nottinghamshire, who later wrote a bestselling book (Emma and I) about her seeing-eye dog. Emma had performed her duties for eleven years when, remarkably, Sheila (who had been born blind) had her sight restored after an operation. Not long after, Emma herself developed cataracts and, when her sight failed, they swapped roles—Sheila Hocken guiding her faithful dog around. Emma died at the ripe old age of 17 in November 1981, having the added distinction of being the oldest guide dog for the blind on record.

Left: The Bulldog is a delightful companion. Sadly, however, it rarely lives beyond eight or nine years. Its walking capacity is about half a mile. It should never be exercised in hot weather.

Below: The perky Yorkshire Terrier may live well into its teens. This show dog is far removed from the pet Yorkies that revel in getting gloriously muddy.

KEEPING SNUG AND WELL

● Old dogs, in common with old people, feel the cold. Make sure that they have adequate heating.
● Toy breeds, and all those with short coats, benefit from the protection of a coat when being exercised in winter.

Care of the Elderly Dog

Above: Dogs can be a great comfort to the elderly. Often they are the remaining link with a lost partner. Regular veterinary check-ups from the age of eight should enable the veterinarian to spot any defect and take action to prolong the ageing pet's life.

Again in common with humans, the dog's organs wear out with age—it may suffer from heart, kidney, and liver failure.

Because of veterinary skills there is no reason to fear that because an elderly dog begins to ail, death is imminent. What is important is that any weakness is detected in time for treatment to be effective.

The dog's hearing and eyesight may, for example, begin to deteriorate slowly from the age of about eight, and it is from this time onwards that regular examinations by your veterinarian are more than ever necessary.

For instance, a little cough that you had disregarded could be the onset of a heart condition, which if caught in time should enable your pet with medication to live out its lifespan.

Because your dog is getting old there is no need to change its routine drastically. If for example, you have taken a walk together at certain times every day, continue to do so, but cut down on the duration of the walks. Similarly, you may find that your dog copes better with two smaller meals than with one large meal a day.

Having an elderly dog to look after is rather like caring for a puppy again. A dog always needs its owner, but the dependence of puppyhood becomes pronounced again in old age.

GROWING OLD TOGETHER

● Should an elderly person keep a dog? What if they should predecease their pet? This is a question that often crops up, particularly in the case of lonely old people who live alone, and would love to have a canine companion.

● Obviously it is ill advised for a frail, elderly person to keep a large, powerful dog. But there is no reason why they should not keep a pet as long as arrangements are made in advance for the animal's welfare in the event of its owner's death.

● Have a chat with the breeder at the time of purchase. Perhaps they will agree to take the dog back. Certainly they will be able to give you the address of the breed rescue society. There are also various animal charities which will undertake to look after a pet for the rest of its natural life in return for a bequest, or lifetime subscription.

DOG BREEDS

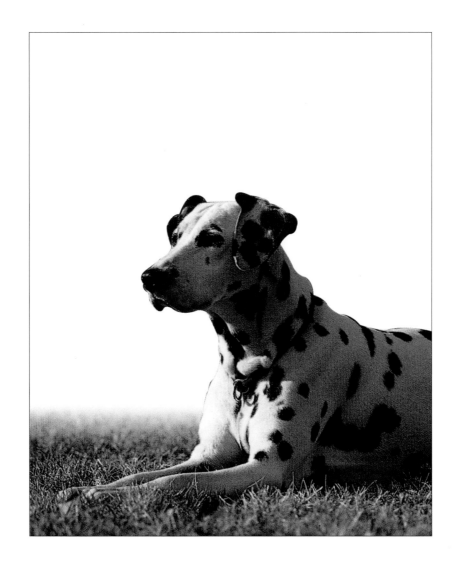

Breeds of the World Introduction

From the time that dogs first became domesticated, they have been selectively bred by humans for different purposes, such as hunting, herding, or guarding. In more recent times they have gradually been bred for more and more specialized tasks, leading to the great diversity of dog breeds recognized today. In the breed descriptions on the following pages, information is provided on the origins and development of each breed, together with its characteristics and temperament, acceptable size range, and color varieties.

AFGHANISTAN
Afghan Hound

AUSTRALIA
Australian Cattle Dog
Australian Silky Terrier
Australian Terrier
Kelpie

AUSTRIA
Austrian Coarse-haired Hound
Austrian Hound
Austrian Short-haired Pinscher
Tyrolean Hound

BALKAN STATES
Balkan Hound
Bosnian Coarse-haired Hound
Charplaninatz
Croatian Shepherd
Dalmatian
Istrian Coarse-haired Hound
Istrian Short-haired Hound
Karst Shepherd
Posavatz Hound
Yugoslavian Mountain Hound
Yugoslavian Tricolor Hound

BELGIUM
Belgian Sheepdog (Groenendael – Malinois. Tervueren – Laekenois)
Bouvier des Ardennes
Bouvier des Flandres (Belgium – France)
Brussels Griffon
Griffon Brabançon
Schipperke
St. Hubert Bloodhound

BRAZIL
Brazilian Guard Dog
Brazilian Tracker

CANADA
Inuit Dog
Landseer
Newfoundland

CHINA
Chow Chow
Pekingese
Shar-Pei

CUBA
Havana Bichon

CZECH REPUBLIC/ SLOVAKIA
Black Forest Hound
Czech (Cesky) Terrier
Czech Coarse-haired Setter
Slovakian Chuvach (Kuvak)

DENMARK
Gammel Dansk Honsehund

EGYPT/ARABIA
Pharaoh Hound
Saluki
Slughi

FINLAND
Finnish Hound
Finnish Spitz
Karelian Bear Dog
Lapponian Herder

FRANCE
Anglo-French White and Black
Anglo-French White and Orange
Anglo-French Tricolor
Ariège Setter
Ariègeois
Artois Hound
Basset Griffon Vendéen
Beauce Shepherd
Bichon Frisé
Billy
Blue Auvergne Setter
Blue Gascony Basset
Bordeaux Mastiff (Dogue de Bordeaux)
Bourbonnais Setter
Briard
Brittany Spaniel
Coarse-haired Griffon
Dupuy Setter
French Setter
French Spaniel
French Tricolor
French White and Black
French White and Orange
Grand Griffon Vendéen
Great Anglo-French Tricolor

Great Anglo-French White and Black
Great Anglo-French White and Orange
Great Gascon of Saintonge
Great Gascony Blue
Levesque
Lowchen
Nivernais Griffon
Norman Artesian Basset
Papillon
Phalène
Picardy Shepherd
Picardy Spaniel
Poitevin
Pont-Audemar Spaniel
Poodle (Germany often credited)
Porcelaine
Pyrenean Mountain Dog (Great Pyrenees)
Pyrenean Smooth-faced Shepherd
Pyrenees Shepherd
Small Anglo-French
Small Blue Gascony Griffon
Small Gascon of Saintonge
Small Gascony Blue
Small-sized French Setter
St. Germain Setter
Tawny Brittany Basset
Tawny Brittany Griffon
Vendéen Griffon Briquet
Wooly-haired Griffon

GERMANY
Affenpinscher
Bavarian Mountain Hound
Boxer
Dachsbracke
Dachshund
Doberman
German Hunt Terrier
German Pointer (Short, Long-haired, Rough)
German Shepherd
German Spaniel
German Spitz
Great Black Spitz
Great Dane
Great Spitz
Great Black Spitz
Great Dane
Hanover Hound

Hovawart
Kromfohrlander
Leonberger
Munsterlander
Pinscher
Pomeranian
Pudelpointer
Rottweiler
Schnauzer (Giant, Standard, Miniature)
Steinbracke
Weimaraner
Westphalian Basset

GREENLAND/ ARCTIC/ FAR NORTH
Greenland Dog
Samoyed

HOLLAND
Drentse Patrijshond (Partridge Dog)
Dutch Setter (Short/ Long-haired)
Dutch Shepherd (Coarse/Smooth-haired)
Keeshond
Stabyhoun
Wetterhoun (Dutch Spaniel)

HUNGARY
Hungarian Coarse-haired Setter
Hungarian Grayhound
Hungarian Vizsla
Komondor
Kuvasz
Mudi
Puli
Pumi
Transylvanian Hound

ISRAEL
Canaan Dog

ITALY
Bergamese Shepherd
Bolognese
Cirneco dell'Etna
Italian Coarse-haired Segugio
Italian Grayhound
Italian Setter
Italian Short-haired Segugio
Italian Spinone
Italian Spitz

Maltese Terrier (controversy whether Malta or Italy)
Maremma Sheepdog
Neopolitan Mastiff

JAPAN
Ainu Dog
Hokkaido Dog
Japanese Akita (Akita Inu)
Japanese Chin (Spaniel)
Japanese Fighting dog
Japanese Spitz
San Shu Dog
Shiba Inu

MEXICO
Chihuahua
Chinese Crested Dog (via China)
Mexican Hairless (Xoloitzcuintli)

MOROCCO
Atlas Dog

NORWAY
Norwegian Sheepdog (Buhund)
Norwegian Elkhound (Gray)
Norwegian Elkhound (Black)
Dunker
Haldenstover
Hygenhund
Lundehund

POLAND
Polish Hound
Tatra Shepherd
Valee Shepherd

PORTUGAL
Castro Laboriere Dog
Estrela Mountain Dog
Portuguese Mountain Dog
Portuguese Podengo (Giant, Medium, Dwarf)
Portuguese Setter
Portuguese Water Dog
Rafeiro do Alentejo

■ RUSSIA
Borzoi

■ SOUTH AFRICA
Basenji
Rhodesian Ridgeback

■ SPAIN
Burgos Setter
Catalonian Shepherd
Ibizan Hound (Smooth,
Coarse, Long-haired)
Pyrenean Mastiff
Spanish Grayhound
Spanish Hound
Spanish Mastif

■ SWEDEN
Drever
Hamiltonstovare –
(Hamilton Hound)
Jamthund
Lapland Spitz
Norrbottenspets
Schillerstovare
(Hound)
Smalandsstovare
Swedish Gray Dog
Vastgotaspets

■ SWITZERLAND
Appenzeller Cattle Dog
Bernese Hound
Bernese Mountain
(Cattle)
Entlebucher Cattle
Dog
Great Swiss Cattle
Dog
Jura Hound
Lucerne Hound
Small Bernese
Hound
Small Jura Hound
Small Lucerne Hound
Small Swiss Hound
St. Bernard
St. Hubert-type Jura
Hound
Swiss Coarse-haired
Hound
Swiss Hound

■ TIBET
Lhasa Apso
Shih Tsu
Tibetan Mastiff
Tibetan Spaniel
Tibetan Terrier

**UNITED KINGDOM
AND IRELAND**
Airedale Terrier
Beagle
Bearded Collie
Bedlington Terrier
Border Collie
Border Terrier
Bull Terrier
Bulldog
Cairn Terrier
Cavalier King Charles
Spaniel
Clumber Spaniel
Curly-coated Retriever
Dandie Dinmont Terrier
Deerhound (Scottish)
English Cocker Spaniel
English Setter
English Springer Spaniel
English Toy Terrier
Field Spaniel
Flat-coated Retriever
Fox Terrier (Smooth)
Fox Terrier (Wire-haired)
Foxhound (English)
French Bulldog
(French also
claim credit)

Golden Retriever
Gordon Setter
Grayhound
Mastiff
Miniature Bull Terrier
Norfolk Terrier
Norwich Terrier
Old English Sheepdog
(Bobtail)
Otterhound
Pointer
Red and White Setter
Rough Collie
Scottish Terrier (Formerly
Aberdeen Terrier)
Sealyham Terrier
Shetland Sheepdog
Skye Terrier
Smooth Collie
Soft-coated Wheaten
Terrier
Staffordshire Bull Terrier
Sussex Spaniel
Welsh Corgi (Cardigan)
Welsh Corgi (Pembroke)
Welsh Springer Spaniel
Welsh Terrier
West Highland White
Terrier

Whippet
Yorkshire Terrier

**UNITED STATES
OF AMERICA**
Alaskan Malamute
American Foxhound
American Staffordshire
Terrier (Pit Bull/Yankee
Terrier)
Basset Hound
Black and Tan
Coonhound
Boston Terrier
Chesapeake Bay Retriever
Siberian Husky

The Dog Classifications: Groups

Dogs are divided into distinct groups according to the purpose for which they have been bred. This aids classification at shows and enables visitors to know when and where their favorite breeds can be found. Reading about the groups also enables the buyer to decide which group includes varieties most suited to their lifestyle—the sportsman, for instance, perhaps scorning the toy group, which might hold tremendous appeal for his wife.

NON-SPORTING GROUP

There is an exception to the obvious naming of groups: the one that is described as "non-sporting." This is reserved for dogs which are not toys and have not been bred for any specific purpose. Many of the traditional pet breeds are to be found in this classification, and so are new breeds and those that may have been newly imported from their country of origin, for which no ready classification can be found.

Many popular pet dogs fall within the non-sporting category, including the Dalmatian, Chow Chow, and Boston Terrier, the Schipperke, and the dignified Keeshond. But bear in mind that, because a breed is in the non-sporting Group today, it may not necessarily be there tomorrow!

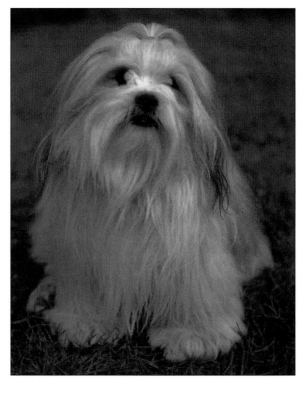

Above: For many centuries the Lhaso Apso existed only in Tibet, where it was used to guard monasteries. It arrived in the West in the 20th century.

Below: The Schipperke comes from the Netherlands, where it was used to guard barges. It makes a good house dog and family pet.

NON-SPORTING GROUP
Bichon Frisé
Boston Terrier
Bulldog
Canaan Dog
Chow Chow
Dalmatian
Finnish Spitz
French Bulldog
German Spitz (Klein)
German Spitz (Mittel)
Japanese Akita
Japanese Spitz
Keeshond
Leonberger
Lhaso Apso
Poodle (Miniature)
Poodle (Standard)
Poodle (Toy)
Schipperke
Tibetan Spaniel
Tibetan Terrier

WORKING GROUP
Akitas
Alaskan Malamute
Anatolian Shepherd Dogs
Bernese Mountain Dog
Boxer
Bullmastiff
Doberman
Giant Schnauzer
Great Dane
Great Pyrenees
Inuit Dog
Komondor
Kuvasz
Mastiff

Above: The Border Collie is among the most popular of working breeds. It originates from Scotland, and is now used all over the world for working with sheep.

Left: The Mastiff is loyal and suspicious of strangers, and is used as a guard dog.

If you are planning to attend a big dog show, one for example, that is run over a number of days—it is particularly important to familiarize yourself with the groups. Non-sporting and toy may for instance be exhibited on one day, and hounds and working breeds on another.

THE WORKING AND HERDING GROUPS

The working and herding groups contains breeds originally bred as guards and protectors of sheep and other livestock. Within these groups, as might be expected, are found the Doberman, German Shepherd and Rottweiler, sheepdogs such as the Border Collie and Old English Sheepdog, and many other breeds designed to perform a guarding and protecting role in their native land.

Some of these breeds, originally bred for ferocity, have, through careful breeding, now emerged as gentle pets. However, it must be remembered that instincts prevail, and that the majority of dogs in this group are happiest and healthiest when they have access to open spaces and a job to do.

Newfoundland
Portuguese Water Dog
Rottweiler
St. Bernard
Samoyed
Schnauzer
Siberian Husky
Swedish Vallhund

HERDING GROUP
Australian Cattle Dogs
Bearded Collies
Belgian Shepherd Dog
(Groenendael)
Belgian Shepherd Dog
(Laekenois)
Belgian Shepherd Dog
(Malinois)

Belgian Shepherd Dog
(Tervuren)
Bouvier Des Flandres
Briard
Collie (Rough)
Collie (Smooth)
German Shepherd Dog
(Alsatian)
Hungarian Puli
Old English Sheepdog
Shetland Sheepdog
Welsh Corgi (Cardigan)
Welsh Corgi (Pembroke)

67

Below: The English Toy Terrier is the toy version of the Manchester Terrier, and is not often seen these days.

Below: The Bichon Frisé is descended from the Barbet (Water Spaniel) from which the word "barbichon" comes. It became a successful circus performer.

TOY GROUP

The toy group comprises those breeds that have been bred solely as diminutive companions, and the traditional lap dogs are to be found in this category. The newcomer will, however, find some surprises. The toy Poodle, for instance, is not in this group, but is to be found alongside the miniature and standard Poodle in the non-sporting group, while the perky Yorkshire Terrier has a place in the toy group and not with his larger terrier relations.

The smallest toy breed is the Chihuahua, the standard weight for which is up to 6lb (2.7kg) with 2–4lb (1–1.8kg) preferred, followed by the Yorkshire Terrier, whose weight should be no more than 7lb (3.1kg). However, it will be appreciated that these and other weights—and indeed heights—are those desired for exhibition purposes, and there are many happy, healthy examples of their breeds which are bigger, smaller, heavier or lighter than their standard dictates.

The largest member of the toy group is the Cavalier King Charles Spaniel, the requirement for which is a well-balanced dog within the range 12–18lb (5.5–8kg).

Don't be misled into thinking that toy dogs are purely ornamental. They enjoy being exercised and make excellent small guards.

TOY GROUP	
Affenpinscher	Miniature Pinscher
Australian Silky Terrier	Papillon
Brussels Griffon	Pekingese
Chihuahua (Long Coat)	Pomeranian
Chihuahua	Pug
(Smooth Coat)	Shih Tzu
Chinese Crested Dog	Silky Terriers
English Toy Spaniel	Yorkshire Terrier
Italian Grayhound	
Japanese Chin	
Maltese	

Above: The Bedlington Terrier was first bred in the 18th and 19th centuries for catching vermin and other small animals. It was particularly popular with poachers.

Above: The Skye Terrier is an old breed that has contributed to the development of many of the Scottish terrier breeds.

THE TERRIER GROUP

The terrier group comprises lively dogs which were predominantly bred to hunt small animals like rats and foxes. They are affectionate and make good pets, but they are extremely lively, bouncy dogs, not averse to the occasional scrap. The terrier would make a first-class companion for the young, but it is not ideally suitable for a sedate, elderly person—although they can be immensely loving.

Terriers come in various sizes, one of the most popular being the West Highland White Terrier, (or "Westie"), a white terrier that stands approximately 11in (28cm) at the withers. The Airedale Terrier is the biggest terrier, 23–24in (58–61cm) bitches are slightly less—as is usually the case.

The Bull Terrier and the Staffordshire Bull Terrier are the least terrier-like in appearance of this group's members, but it must be borne in mind that the Bull Terrier has an extinct white terrier in its makeup, while the "Staffy" descends from Bulldog–Terrier stock.

TERRIER GROUP	Manchester Terrier
Airedale Terrier	Miniature Schnauzer
American Staffordshire	Norfolk Terrier
Terriers	Norwich Terrier
Australian Terrier	Parson Jack Russell Terrier
Bedlington Terrier	Scottish Terrier
Border Terrier	Sealyham Terrier
Bull Terrier	Skye Terrier
Cairn Terrier	Soft-Coated
Dandie Dinmont Terrier	Wheaten Terrier
Fox Terrier (Smooth)	Staffordshire Bull Terrier
Fox Terrier (Wire)	Welsh Terrier
Irish Terrier	West Highland
Kerry Blue Terrier	White Terrier
Lakeland Terrier	

It is a common mistake to mix up the West Highland White Terrier with the Scottish Terrier, the latter being in fact an all-black dog, once known as the Aberdeen Terrier.

THE SPORTING DOG GROUP

Sporting dogs, designed to retrieve game birds and water fowl are, in the main, gentle, companionable animals that combine admirably the role of sportsperson's dog and household pet—such as the Golden Retriever and the Labrador Retriever.

Again, there is a great variety of sporting dogs to choose from, ranging from the Cocker Spaniel (the "Merry Cocker") to the bigger setters, retrievers, and pointers.

The setter is bred to "set," to stand rigid on scenting game so that its master may detect the presence of prey. The pointer "points" by its stance toward the position of the game, and the retriever, as one might expect, retrieves shot game from land and also from water.

The job of the spaniel is to flush birds from their cover and to retrieve. The spaniel, however, has undertaken innumerable tasks, and evidence exists that spaniels were being taught to set as long ago as the 13th century.

Above: A sleepy wirehaired pointer belies the alertness demonstrated when it comes "on point"—indicating the quarry during a hunt.

Below: Spaniels are descended from Spanish dogs and are used both to flush out and to retrieve game.

SPORTING GROUP	Spaniel (American Cocker)
Brittany Spaniel	Spaniel (Clumber)
English Setter	Spaniel (Cocker)
German Short-haired	Spaniel (English Springer)
Pointer	Spaniel (Field)
German Wire-haired	Spaniel (Irish Water)
Pointer	Spaniel (Sussex)
Gordon Setter	Spaniel (Welsh Springer)
Hungarian Vizsla	Weimaraner
Irish Red and White	
Setters	
Italian Spinone	
Large Munsterlander	
Pointer	
Retriever	
(Chesapeake Bay)	
Retriever (Curly-coated)	
Retriever (Flat-coated)	
Retriever (Golden)	
Retriever (Labrador)	

THE HOUND GROUP

Hounds were bred to hunt by sight or scent, hence the terms "scent hounds" and "gaze hounds." Scent hounds, such as the Beagle, Basset, and Bloodhound, use their noses to seek out their prey. The Afghan Hound, Saluki, and Grayhound to name a few, are gaze hounds which hunt their prey with the aid of their exceptional sight.

There are many hound breeds to choose from, ranging from the Miniature Dachshund to the Grayhound, Bloodhound, or Whippet.

With the exception of foxhounds, which inevitably belong to a foxhunting pack, and possibly the Otterhound and Beagle, hounds generally make good household pets. However, they have the instinct to wander, and are unsuitable for those who cannot offer space and a very well fenced garden.

Bassets in particular have a propensity to roam. Owners have been known to receive telephone calls from many miles distant asking them to come and collect their dog.

Of all the dog types, hounds have the longest association with humans, having been the first to be used by early people for hunting.

Above: The Borzoi is a very swift hound that was used in Russia for wolf hunting. It hunts by sight rather than scent.

Below: Few Basset packs exist today. In the past they were used for hunting hares, and would catch their quarry through persistence rather than speed.

HOUND GROUP	
Afghan Hound	Foxhound
Basenji	Grayhound
Basset Fauve de Bretagne	Harriers
Basset Hound	Ibizan Hound
Beagle	Irish Wolfhound
Bloodhound	Otterhound
Borzoi	Petit Basset Griffon
Dachshund (Long-haired)	Vendéen
Dachshund (Miniature Long-haired)	Pharaoh Hound
	Rhodesian Ridgeback
Dachshund (Smooth-haired)	Saluki
	Whippet
Dachshund (Miniature Smooth-haired)	
Dachshund (Wire-haired)	
Dachshund (Miniature Wire-haired)	
Deerhound	
Elkhound	

The Poodle

The glamor of the show Poodle in its elegant lion clip tends to overshadow its versatility. It is a playful, exuberant dog, and a successful competitor in obedience. As a companion, it is intelligent and (particularly the standard) hardy, and a good retriever. It is also a great imitator, which is why Poodles are so often chosen to perform tricks in circuses. They are quick learners.

The Poodle in fact originated as a water retriever and is believed to have evolved from the French Barbet, with its curly, wooly coat, and the Hungarian Water Hound. While it is generally supposed to be a French breed, it originated in Germany the word "Poodle" coming from the German *pudelnass* or puddle. In France it is known as the *Caniche*, this word coming from the French *canard* which means duck. Poodles were great retrievers of ducks.

The miniature and toy Poodle varieties have of course evolved from the standard.

The Poodle has Royal connections. "Boy," the inseparable companion of Prince Rupert of the Rhine in the English Civil War (1642–49), was credited with mystical powers. A pamphlet concerning this Poodle is preserved in the Bodleian Library in Oxford, England and describes how Prince Rupert, with the dog sitting on a table by his side, would frequently turn and kiss it during Council debate. The dog was killed at the Battle of Marston Moor (1644).

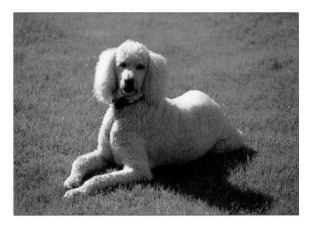

Above: The standard Poodle. The Poodle was once highly valued as a water retriever, although it is seldom used in that role anymore.

Varieties: From left to right: black, white, apricot, brown, cream, silver, and blue.

Left: The toy Poodle is descended from the standard. This example has the black nose, lips, eye rims, and nails that are desirable with white or cream coats.

KEY FACTS

Character: High-spirited and good-natured. Excellent show dog.

Exercise: Varies with size. The standard is particularly active. Miniatures and toys are more suitable for town-dwellers.

Grooming: Needs regular clipping. The lion clip is obligatory for showing. Preparation takes time.

Feeding: The standard would require approximately 1½ cans (14oz/400g size) of a branded meaty product, with biscuit added in equal part by volume. (Toy and miniature, ¼–½ can respectively. But all dogs are individuals!)

Longevity: Many Poodles live well into their teens.

Faults: Include eyes set too close together, tail curled, or carried over back.

THE FRENCH CONNECTION

The French queen, Marie Antoinette, is credited with the design of the famous lion clip, which she believed should match the livery of her servants.

Poodles should have almond-shaped eyes and may be any solid color. However, white and creams should have black noses, lips and eye-rims; black toenails are desirable. Apricots should have dark eyes with black points or deep amber eyes with liver points. Blacks, silvers and blues should have black nose, lips, eye-rims and toenails, and creams, apricots, browns, silvers and blues may show variations of the same color up to the age of 18 months.

There is no difference between the three Poodle varieties except in size. Standard: height at shoulder over 15in (38cm); miniature: shoulder height at under 38cm (15in) but not under 11in (28cm); toy: height at shoulder under 11in (28cm).

The Shar-Pei: (Chinese fighting dog)

Varieties: From top to bottom: fawn, black, red, and cream.

KEY FACTS

Character: Alert, active, calm and independent. Affectionate and devoted.

Exercise: Was a wild boar hunter, so needs plenty of it.

Grooming: Use fairly stiff brush. Rub down with towel or hound glove.

Feeding: Approximately 1½ cans (14oz/400g size) of a branded meaty product, with biscuit added in equal part by volume. (Note in all instances: if your dog is over or under the standard weight for its breed, consult your veterinary surgeon.)

Longevity: Average.

Faults: Include any sign of irritation of eyeball, conjunctiva or eyelids.

It is not long since the Shar-Pei graced the *Guinness Book of Pet Records* in the World's Rarest Dog slot, but today it has a growing band of devotees in the United States (although the America Kennel Club has not yet recognized the breed), Canada, and in the United Kingdom.

Despite being bred as a fighting dog, the Shar-Pei is an amiable dog unless provoked. Indeed it is believed that drugs were used to promote aggression, while the breed's success as a fighter was largely due to its folds of loose skin, which made it difficult for an adversary to catch hold.

ORIGINS

Likenesses of the Shar-Pei survive from the Han Dynasty (206BC–AD220), and it is possible that it originated in Tibet or the northern provinces of China some 2,000 years ago.

The future of the Shar-Pei was in peril in 1947, when the People's Republic of China put such a heavy tax on dogs that very few people could keep them. It is fortunate that a number of fine specimens were smuggled out of China.

The dog, which has wrinkles not unlike those of the Bloodhound, stands only 18–20in (46–51cm) high at the withers and weighs up to 50lb (22.5kg). It comes in solid colors: black, red, light or dark shades of fawn, and cream.

The Chow Chow

KEY FACTS

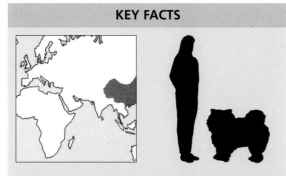

Character: Beautiful and aloof, this companion and guard reserves its affection for the family.
Exercise: It appreciates a fair amount of exercise.
Grooming Use a wire brush, a few minutes daily. An hour-long grooming at weekends works wonders.
Feeding: Approximately 1–1½ cans (14oz/400g size) of a branded meaty product, with biscuit added in equal part by volume.
Longevity: Average.
Faults: Include any artificial shortening of the coat which alters the natural outline or expression.

The beautiful Chow Chow, with its distinctive blue tongue, is a lion-like member of the Spitz family, known for over 2,000 years. It is certainly one of the oldest Spitz varieties and was possibly the original Lama's Mastiff.

This breed had many roles, including those of guard, hunter, and sled dog. It has also been bred for its flesh, which is still considered a delicacy in the Far East.

Once known as the Tartar Dog, and also as the Dog of the Barbarians, the Chow Chow has always—rather like the Shar-Pei—had an undeserved reputation for ferocity. It can indeed give a good account of itself, but it is unlikely to pick a fight.

Chow Chows, which have a unique, stilted gait, come in parti-colored black, red, blue, fawn, cream, or white—frequently shaded, but not in patches or parti-colored (the under-part of the tail and the backs of the thighs are frequently of a lighter color). Dogs stand 19–22in (48–56cm) high at the shoulder, bitches 18–20in (46–51cm).

Varieties: From top to bottom: fawn, black, cream, red, white, and blue.

The Schnauzer

Like the Dalmatian, Basenji, and several other breeds, the Schnauzer gets on well with horses and, in the days of the stagecoach in Central Europe, would run alongside the horses and sleep by the coachman's side at night. It has been used as a messenger in the armed services, is an excellent ratter, and a keen, obedient dog. However, the main role of this attractive breed today is as an amusing, intelligent companion. Incidentally, the Miniature Schnauzer was derived from crossing the smallest breed members with another German dog, the Affenpinscher. It is thought that the Schnauzer itself originated by crossing a black German Poodle with a gray Spitz.

The Giant Schnauzer, the dog of which stands 25½–27½in (65–70cm) high, and bitches 23½–25½in (60–65cm) was in fact first exhibited in Germany in 1879 under the name Coarse-haired Pinscher (*Pinscher* is German for "terrier"). In Munich in October 1909, it was referred to as the Russian Bear Schnauzer, and has been used for police work.

The standard Schnauzer stands ideally at 19in (48.5cm) at the withers, with bitches 18in (45.5cm); the miniature should be 14in (35.5cm), bitches 13in (33cm).

Standard Schnauzer

Above: The Giant Schnauzer showing pure black markings. It was once used as a cattle dog and is an intelligent and playful companion.

Varieties: from left to right: black, dark gray, light gray, and black and silver.

KEY FACTS

Character: Robust and good with children. Playful, yet a fine guard.

Exercise: Likes plenty. Will follow horses. Useful, obedient dog.

Grooming: Use wire brush daily. Comb whiskers. Coat needs stripping twice a year.

Feeding: Miniature: ½–¾ cans (14oz/400g size); standard: 1–1½ cans; giant: at least 2½ cans of a branded meaty product with biscuit added in equal part by volume.

Longevity: Good.

Faults: Include any white markings on head, chest and legs.

Schnauzers were first seen in Baden-Württemberg and Bavaria and have long been popular in northern Switzerland and France. They much prefer living indoors with the family to life in an outside kennel.

MARKINGS AND COLORINGS

Colors are pure black (white markings on head, chest, and legs being deemed undesirable) or salt and pepper shades ranging from dark iron-gray to light gray. The miniature comes in all salt and pepper colors in even proportions, or pure black, or black and silver (solid black with silver markings on eyebrow, muzzle, chest, and brisket, and on the forelegs below the point of the elbow, on the inside of the hind legs below the stifle joint, on the vent, and under the tail).

Below: Miniature Schnauzers were created by crossing small Schnauzers with the Affenpinscher. They are less aggressive than the larger varieties.

The French Bulldog

The "Frenchie" has long had a reputation for attaching itself to ladies and it has been the pet of many actresses, writers, and ladies of fashion. However, it has no mean number of male devotees who enjoy its companionship and macho image.

BAD TEMPER

Intelligent and devoted, it generally gets on well with other pets but beware lest its temper should be aroused. A word of reprimand, however, and it will slink away and sulk. The "Frenchie" simply hates to be out of favor!

An ideal companion and show dog—although somewhat heavy to lift onto the show table. They stand at 12–14in (30–35cm); dogs are 28lb (12.5kg) in weight; bitches 24lb (11kg). The development of the breed is generally credited to the French who are said to have crossed small bulldogs taken to France by lace makers from Nottingham, England, in the 19th century,

KEY FACTS

Character: Full of courage, yet with clown-like qualities. Devoted. Intelligent.
Exercise: Moderate. Not in very hot weather.
Grooming: Use fairly stiff brush daily. Rub down with hound glove or towel. Lubricate facial creases.
Feeding: Approximately ¾ can (14oz/400g size) of a branded meaty product, with biscuit added in equal part by volume.
Longevity: Short to moderate.
Faults: Include showing white of eye when looking straight ahead.

with dogs imported to France from Spain. However, other sources would have it that the French developed the breed by mating a little-known French variety with Belgian imported breeds. In any event, the bat ears and short, undocked screwtail are essential features of the breed.

"Frenchies," although not easily obtainable, have a large, enthusiastic band of followers—and rightly so—and always draw an appreciative show audience. They come in brindle, pied, or fawn.

Varieties: From left to right: fawn, brindled, and pied.

The Dalmatian

Varieties: From top to bottom: liver spotted and black spotted.

KEY FACTS

Character: Outgoing, friendly. Capable of endurance and speed.

Exercise: A traditional coach dog needing plenty of exercise.

Grooming: Daily brush and rub down. Easy to care for but beware: neglect grooming and this pet will deposit white hair on the carpet.

Feeding: 1½–2 cans (14oz/400g size) of a branded meaty product with biscuit added in equal part by volume.

Longevity: Good.

Faults: Include patches, tricolors, and lemon spots. Also bronzing on spots in adults.

The Dalmatian was something of a status symbol in 18th-century England when widely used as a carriage or coach dog. It is generally believed that the breed originated in the Balkans, although friezes discovered in Greece and the Middle East depict a similar dog.

THE ALL-PURPOSE DOG

The Dalmatian is a fine all-purpose dog: coach dog, ratter, retriever, and draft dog. Today, however, it is mainly kept as a much-loved household pet.

An important point: when buying a Dalmatian puppy, drop a set of keys behind it to test for its reaction. Alas, there is a tendency to deafness in this breed. The desired height of the Dalmatian is 23–24in (58.4–61cm), with bitches 22–23in (55.9–58.4cm).

The ground color is always pure white. Black spotted has dense black spots, and liver spotted has liver brown spots. The spots should not run together, and should be round and well distributed.

The Japanese Spitz

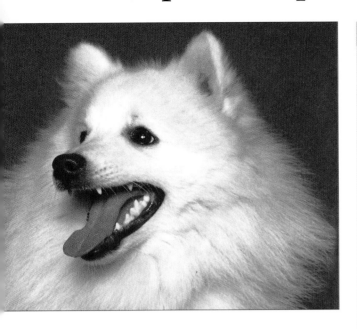

KEY FACTS

Character: Affectionate and companionable but tends to be wary of strangers.
Exercise: A natural herder, enjoys freedom but will adapt to its owner's requirements.
Grooming: Daily with a stiff brush.
Feeding: 1 can (14oz/400g size) of a branded meaty product, with biscuit added in equal part by volume.
Longevity: Good to average.
Faults: Include ears too wide apart.

Above left: The Japanese Spitz. Pure white is the only acceptable color.

Below: The Finnish Spitz, one of the Spitz varieties from which the Japanese Spitz is descended. The Spitz dogs have one of the oldest ancestries in the dog world.

The Japanese Spitz is a comparative newcomer outside its native land as both family pet and show dog, but is fast gaining a band of devotees.

To discuss the background of the Japanese Spitz one must look to its close relative the Nordic or Norrbotten Spitz as they have the same origins.

The breed's ancestor, the Norrbotten Spitz, is also little known outside its native Sweden. It was in fact declared extinct in 1948 but there was renewed interest in the 1960s, resulting in sufficient registrations for the breed to become re-established. These Spitz varieties no doubt derived from Finnish Spitz or Norwegian Buhund ancestry.

The Japanese Spitz was developed as a separate breed in Japan, and is not unlike the Pomeranian (another Spitz variety) but with a larger frame.

The Japanese Spitz stands 12–14in (30–36cm), bitches slightly less, and the only allowable color is pure white. It has a pointed muzzle, triangular ears standing erect, and a bushy tail curled over its back, characteristic of all the Spitz breeds.

KEEPING THE SPITZ IN CHECK

This is a sharp little dog, inclined to be yappy if unchecked: it is perhaps best as the devoted companion of a single person or a couple, rather than with a family and young children.

Right: The Norwegian Buhund, from which the Japanese Spitz is partly descended, was used as a cattle dog and also makes a good guard dog.

The Bernese Mountain Dog

This beautiful animal is the best known of the four Swiss mountain dogs. The others are the Great Swiss Sennenhund, the Appenzell Sennenhund, and the Entlebuch Sennenhund.

In Switzerland, Bernese Mountain Dogs are extensively used for draft purposes, and it is not unusual to see a Bernese Mountain Dog pulling milk churns up the mountain side. In some countries (in the United Kingdom, for instance) it is illegal to use dogs in this way, but owners get great enjoyment from harnessing up their pets for off-highway events, such as local fêtes, where they frequently raise money for charity.

A large dog—25–27½in (64–70cm), bitches 23–26in (58–66cm)—the Bernese is not all that dissimilar to a very large Border Collie. In fact, however, its origins lie in ancient Rome.

Two thousand years ago, when Roman legions crossed the Alps into northern Europe, they were accompanied by war and guard dogs. From survivors of the latter, four large Alpine breeds evolved: three as sheep-herders, the fourth, the Bernese Mountain Dog, as a draft dog. It takes its name from Berne, where the inhabitants, many of them weavers, would drive their wares to market in a dog cart.

Above: The Pyrenean Mountain Dog is immensely powerful and at one time was used in battle. Today, however, it is known for its gentle, loyal nature.

KEY FACTS

Character: A multipurpose farm dog, capable of draft work. An ideal family pet in the right environment.

Exercise: This is not a town dog. It needs plenty of exercise.

Grooming: Regular brushing or coat will shed.

Feeding: Approximately 2 cans (14oz/400g size) of a branded meaty product with biscuit added in equal part by volume.

Longevity: Average.

Faults: Any sign of aggression, which must not be tolerated.

THE OUTDOOR LIFE

The Bernese makes an excellent family pet in the right environment. It needs space and exercise. It would be cruel to keep it in an apartment. It also prefers cold weather and, while many breed members do live indoors, they come to no harm being kenneled outside.

The breed tends to devote itself to one person, but will adapt to share its tremendous loyalty with the family.

The coat of the Bernese should be jet black, with rich reddish brown on cheeks, over the eyes, and on all four legs and chest. There is a slight to medium sized symmetrical white head marking (blaze) and white chest marking (cross), which are essential. White paws are preferred, but are not essential.

The Rottweiler

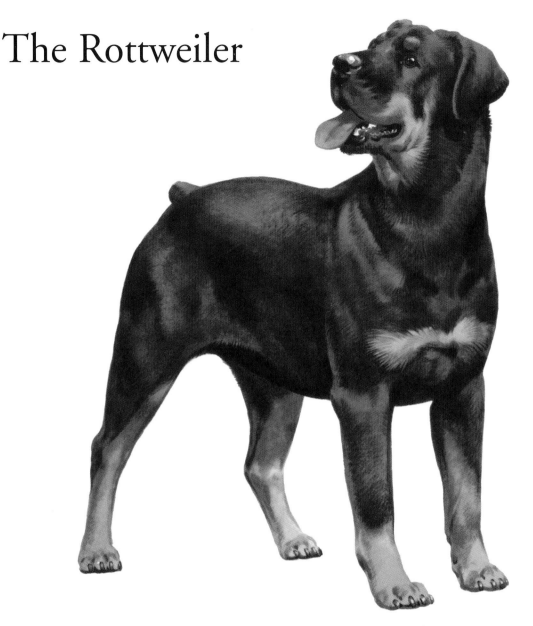

The Rottweiler is a splendid animal which in recent times has received adverse publicity, largely through breed members having fallen into unsuitable, inexperienced hands.

The Rottweiler has been known since the Middle Ages, when it was a hunter of wild boar, and has developed into a trusted cattle dog. It comes from the German town of Rottweil in Württemberg where—known as the Rottweiler Metzgerhund or Rottweil Butcher's Dog—it was frequently used for draft purposes and would pull the butchers' carts. It has also been used as a police dog and guard in the armed services.

A LOYAL COMPANION

The Rottweiler is a natural guard and protector and extremely loyal to its master, and its master's family—and other pets—if it has been brought up with them. It does however require knowledgeable handling and obedience training, and to provoke it into aggression is sheer stupidity bearing in mind the strength of this dog, and the fact that it rarely gives any warning of attack.

Sadly too much emphasis has been placed on the breed's macho image and too little on its abilities as for example, a sled dog, mountain rescue dog, and obedience competitor.

KEY FACTS

Character: Bold, courageous and loyal. Working dog and guard. Not recommended for the inexperienced.
Exercise: This former wild boar hunter and cattle dog needs an outlet for its energies.
Grooming: Regular brushing.
Feeding: Approximately 2–2½ cans (14oz/400g size) of a branded meaty product with biscuit added in equal part by volume.
Longevity: Average.
Faults: Fearsome if provoked.

Above: The Rottweiler should be black with markings that range from tan to mahogany in color.

The Rottweiler stands 25–27in (63–69cm) high, bitches 23–25in (58–63.5cm). Its color is always black with clearly defined markings including a spot over each eye. Markings range from rich tan to mahogany and should not exceed 10 percent of body color.

Left: The Rottweiler is a former hunting dog that is widely used by the police and armed services. Here, a dog is being trained for police duties.

85

The Great Dane

Left: This Great Dane has a fawn coat, one of several color varieties.

The magnificent Great Dane is slow to anger and good with children and other pets. However, because of its sheer size, it is boisterous when young and needs disciplining if it is not to get the upper hand. A weekly visit to the dog training club with this breed would be time well invested.

Acknowledged as a German breed, the Great Dane is believed to be a descendant of the Molossus hounds of Roman times. These were dogs that hunted wild boar, baited bulls, and acted as bodyguards, but there is little of this aggression apparent in the present-day Great Dane.

"APOLLO OF THE DOG WORLD"

Bismarck (1815–98), who had a penchant for the Mastiff, took an interest in the breed and produced a Dane similar to the type we know today by crossing the Mastiff of southern Germany with the Great Dane of the north. This dog was first exhibited at Hamburg in 1863 and by 1866 it had become known as the *Deutsche Dogge* and was referred to as the national Dog of Germany. It is often called the "Apollo of the dog world."

The minimum size of a Great Dane over 18 months of age should be 30in (76cm), bitches 28in (71cm).

Varieties: From left to right: fawn, blue, harlequin, black, and brindle.

Below: The Neapolitan Mastiff's ancestry can be traced back 2,500 years. It is an effective guard dog.

KEY FACTS

Character: Devoted, good-natured and easy to train—but not cheap to feed!
Exercise: Ideally, miles of walking on hard ground every day, if you haven't the land to give it freedom.
Grooming: Daily grooming with a body brush.
Feeding: Up to 4 cans (14oz/400g size) of a branded meaty product, with biscuit added in equal part by volume.
Longevity: Short. Average eight or nine years.
Faults: A little boisterous when young. Any roughness in coat.

There is a number of colors including brindle, fawn, blue, black, and the distinctive harlequin (a pure white underground with all-black or all-blue patches).

One of the saddest things about owning a Great Dane is the knowledge that it has only a short lifespan, for those that attain eight or nine years have done well, and in their latter years they have a tendency to suffer from heart complaints and stiff joints. However, such is the devotion that many owners have for this breed that they feel even a few years are worthwhile.

Great Dane

87

The Doberman

Above: The Doberman can be black, as here, or brown, blue or fawn, with rust markings.

Left: The Doberman is a loyal and devoted pet, and has very strong guarding instincts.

The Doberman was bred as a fearsome guard. Indeed Louis Dobermann of Apolda in Thuringia, Germany, the man from whom the breed took its name, was a tax collector in the 1880s with a penchant for fierce dogs. He wanted the ideal animal to accompany him on his rounds, not a difficult task as he was keeper of the local dog pound, with access to innumerable strays. Intent on breeding for courage, alertness and stamina, Dobermann introduced the Rottweiler to the German Pinscher, and (it is believed) the Manchester Terrier as well, and possibly even the Pointer.

Despite its strong guarding instincts, and provided it receives sufficient training, the Doberman can become a reliable family pet. It is a good tracker, police dog, and just the animal to have guarding a stable or other rural property.

The Doberman stands 27in (69cm), bitches 25½in (65cm),and comes in definite black, brown, blue, or fawn (Isabella) only, with rust-red markings. Incidentally, white markings of any kind are highly undesirable.

KEY FACTS

Character: An alert, aloof guard. Loyal and devoted to owner.

Exercise: The ideal dog for a stable yard or environment offering unfettered freedom.

Grooming: Daily rub-down with terry cloth. This will remove surplus hair.

Feeding: Approximately 1½–2½ cans (14oz/400g size) of a branded meaty product, with biscuit added in equal part by volume.

Longevity: Good.

Faults: Include a possible tendency to overguard.

Left: The Doberman probably contains some Manchester Terrier blood in its ancestry.

Varieties: From left to right: black, brown, blue, and fawn.

The Siberian Husky

Capable of great speed and endurance, the Siberian Husky is a medium-sized working sled dog with a long history of friendship with man. It is also good with children. However, it is a breed that needs space and training if it is not to wander off and molest livestock or become destructive.

This is a dog that will not refuse to leave the fireside in wintertime. In fact, the colder it is the better for this animal. It was bred by the nomadic Chukchi tribes of northeast Asia with the aim of producing a hardy dog which could combine the roles of companion and hunter and those of a speedy sled dog.

It now draws appreciative audiences at dog shows, is used as a search and rescue dog, and is linked worldwide with the sport of sled dog racing.

It originated from the Kolyma River region of Siberia, which extends eastward to the Bering Strait, and was first imported into Alaska in 1909.

The Siberian Husky weighs in at 45–60lb (20–27kg), bitches 35–50lb (16–23kg). It comes in all colors and markings, including white. A variety of markings on the head is common and there include many striking patterns not found in other breeds.

Below: The Alaskan Malamute, like the Husky, is a Spitz breed. It is stronger than the Husky and can pull heavier loads.

KEY FACTS

Character: Reliable, medium-sized working sled dog.
Exercise: This dog has considerable endurance and a great turn of speed. Not suitable for a small home.
Grooming: Daily brushing and combing. Toweling after coat has got wet. Coat sheds once a year, when surplus hair will need combing out.
Feeding: 1½–2½ cans (14oz/400g size) of a branded meaty product, with biscuit added in equal part by volume.
Longevity: Good to average.
Faults: Include a tendency to wander. Can be destructive.

This is a dog that does not display aggression toward strangers or other dogs, but is somewhat reserved in maturity; dogs stand 21–23½in (53–60cm), and bitches 20–22in (51–56cm).

Below: A Siberian Husky pup. Huskies are tireless, willing workers, and make devoted companions.

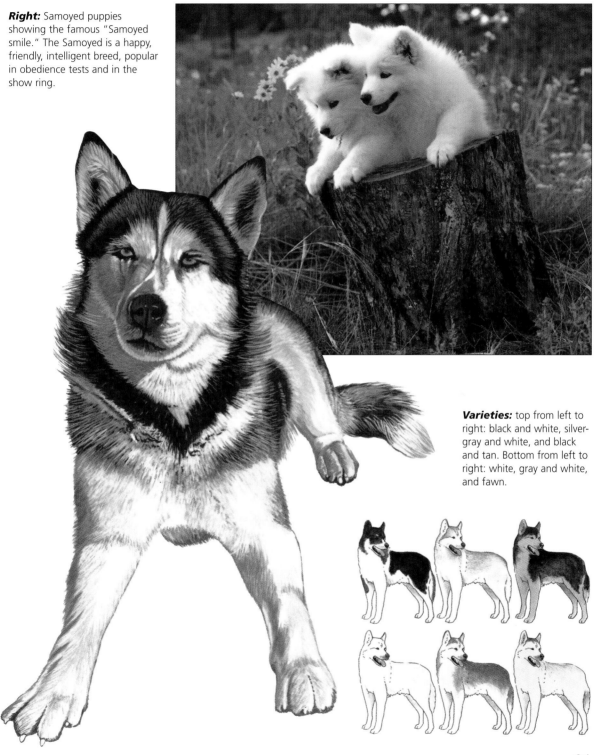

Right: Samoyed puppies showing the famous "Samoyed smile." The Samoyed is a happy, friendly, intelligent breed, popular in obedience tests and in the show ring.

Varieties: top from left to right: black and white, silver-gray and white, and black and tan. Bottom from left to right: white, gray and white, and fawn.

The Newfoundland

A gentle giant, capable of hard work, but suitable as a house pet as long as there is sufficient space. The Newfoundland gets along well with other pets, and may be kept even with toy varieties.

Just as the Border Collie has the natural instinct to round up anything that moves, the Newfoundland has the instinct to swim out to sea and rescue anything in the water, swimming back with it safely to shore.

The breed originates from the northeast of Canada, into whose harbors fishing boats would frequently arrive to avoid bad weather. It is thought that such ships' dogs mated with local dogs whose ancestors included native American dogs and Basque sheepdogs, to produce the Newfoundland.

This is the dog beloved of the poet Byron, whose Newfoundland, "Boatswain", is buried in the grounds of his former home, Newstead Abbey. It also became famous through the paintings of Sir Edward Landseer (1802–73) from whom the Landseer variety, with black and white markings, takes its name.

The average height of the Newfoundland is 28in (71cm), bitches 26in (66cm), while its weight is 140–150lb (64–68kg), bitches 110–120lb (50–54kg).

Colors permitted are black, brown, and "Landseer."

KEY FACTS

Character: Excellent guard, fine swimmer, marvelous with children and other animals.
Exercise: Regular exercise on hard ground.
Grooming: Daily brushing with a hard brush.
Feeding: At least 2½ cans (14oz/400g size) of a branded meaty product, with biscuit added in equal part by volume.
Longevity: Average.
Faults: Include tails with a kink, or curled over back.

Varieties: From left to right: black, brown, and Landseer.

The Mastiff

The Mastiff is an ancient and powerful guard dog, already found in Britain when Julius Caesar landed in 55BC. It is said that, at that time, the Mastiff was fighting alongside his British masters. Thereafter the Romans took a number of these powerful dogs back with them to fight in the arenas of Rome.

There are, however, sources that credit the Mastiff with eastern origins, believing that its ancestry traces back to Tibetan Mastiffs.

It should be noted that the Mastiff is an entirely different breed from the Bull Mastiff, which is a cross between a Mastiff and an English Bulldog. The Mastiff is the larger of the two.

The Mastiff, as a former guard dog and war dog, was undoubtedly bred for violence. This has been bred out so that today the Mastiff is a brave and friendly companion, good with children, albeit sometimes wary with strangers. However, it is not a "beginner's dog" and it would be foolish with a dog of this size not to invest considerable time in training.

KEY FACTS

Character: Brave, intelligent, and loyal.
Exercise: Needs plenty. Best kept on a farm or estate.
Grooming: Daily brushing.
Feeding: 2½ cans (14oz/400g size) of a branded meaty product, with biscuit added in equal part by volume.
Longevity: Average.
Faults: A tendency to lameness. Check with veterinarian for soundness.

The Mastiff stands 30in (76cm) high, bitches 27½in (70cm). Colors are apricot-fawn, silver-fawn, or dark fawn brindle. In all cases, muzzle, ears, eyes, and nose should be black with round orbits, with the black extending upward between them.

Varieties: From top to bottom: fawn, brindle, and silver.

The Boxer

For the family with young children, the boxer is an excellent choice. It is fairly exuberant, and takes a long time to grow up, but generally fits in well with the average family, particularly if there is someone able to take it for long country walks. However, in summer it should not be taken for walks in the heat of the day. Boxers can also be trained for obedience and have been used by the police, in the armed forces and as guide dogs for the blind.

The Boxer's ancestry goes back to the "holding" dogs of Molossus (Mastiff) type, taken into battle against the wild Cimbrians by the Romans. The jaw, like that of the Bulldog, is undershot—a common trait in bull-baiters. The Brabant Bull-baiter, from which the English Bulldog evolved, also had a hand in the evolution of the Boxer.

The Boxer stands 22½–25in (57–63cm) high, bitches 21–23in (53–59cm), and comes in fawn or brindle. The all-white Boxer, which makes an attractive pet, is unacceptable in the show ring. The ears are cropped in many countries.

Above: A pair of Boxers with cropped ears. This procedure, which is common in the US and Europe, makes the ears stand up tall and pointed.

Left: Boxers are descended from the mastiffs, such as the Bull Mastiff, which has the characteristic undershot jaw and powerful body.

KEY FACTS

Character: Brave, clownish, marvelous with children. Not averse to a scrap with other dogs.
Exercise: Enjoys unleashing its boundless energy.
Grooming: Daily brushing.
Feeding: 1½–2½ cans (14oz/400g size) of a branded meaty product, with biscuit added in equal part by volume.
Longevity: Fairly good.
Faults: Include enjoying a scrap; it goes in with its stumpy tail wagging.

Varieties: From top to bottom, amber, brindle, and deer red.

The St. Bernard

This gentle giant makes an ideal family pet for those with the room to accommodate it. Care must, however, be taken to select a St. Bernard pup from a kennel renowned for producing stock both free of hip dysplasia (to which the breed is prone) and with the good temperament for which it is renowned.

The breed takes its name from the refuge of St. Bernard in the Alps, founded shortly before the year AD1000 by a young nobleman, Bernard of Montjoux. Its purpose was to give shelter to travelers over the pass, and those who might have become buried in the snow.

Above: The Anatolian Sheepdog is agile and strong. It is easy to train, but is suspicious of strangers, making it a good guard dog.

KEY FACTS

Character: Calm, sensible, trustworthy, and courageous. Mountain rescue dog.
Exercise: Plenty. However, not too much before adulthood.
Grooming: Regular combing and brushing to keep coat in good condition and avoid shedding.
Feeding: At least 2½ cans (14oz/400g size) of a branded meaty product, with biscuit added in equal part by volume.
Longevity: Not long-lived.
Faults: Chest should never project below elbows. Subject to hip deformities.

Varieties: From left to right: orange, mahogany, and brindle.

feeding costs, one does not see too many St. Bernards, but those that there are generally of good quality.

The color of the St. Bernard may be orange, mahogany, brindle (or red-brindle), or white with patches on the body of any of the aforementioned colors. Markings include a white muzzle, white blaze on face, white collar, white chest, white forelegs, feet and end of tail, black shadings on face and ears.

Often told is the story of Barry, a breed member at the famous hospice that, between 1800 and 1810, is credited with saving no less than 40 lives. However, the St. Bernard tends to be associated by most people with a famous brand of brandy, which for many years they have been used to advertize.

Following Bernard's death, the refuge continued to offer hospitality, but it was not until the middle of the 17th century that the monks, who by then ran the refuge, made the decision to enlist the aid of dogs capable of withstanding the rigors of the Alps to rescue travelers.

Some sources credit the monks with having crossed German Mastiffs with Pyrenean Mountain Dogs to create the St. Bernard. More likely, it is a descendant of the Tibetan Mastiff.

The breed faced extinction around 1820, but a dedicated band of dog fanciers continued breeding and were successful in producing the fine dog we know today.

There are, in fact, two types of St. Bernard: long-haired and short-haired. The monks concentrated on short-haired stock, because snow can gather in long hair and form heavy icicles, impeding the dogs' work.

BIG IS BEAUTIFUL

Because of their sheer size—there is no standard laid down but the taller they are, the better in show terms, provided symmetry is maintained—and resultant

Above: The Estrela Mountain Dog is tough and rugged. Although calm with its owner, it is suspicious of strangers. Although originally a sheepdog, it is also a good guard dog.

The Komondor

KEY FACTS

Character: Excellent guard. Wary of strangers. Not for the inexperienced, but immensely loyal to owner.

Exercise: Puppies are particularly active. Adults need a good amount of exercise, which must be on a leash if in a town.

Grooming: The Komondor has a thick, double coat. The undercoat is soft and wooly, the outer coat long, coarse and wavy. The coat forms in tassel-like cords which are never brushed and combed, although matting has to be avoided.

Feeding: At least 2½ cans (14oz/400g size) of a branded meaty product. with biscuit added in equal part by volume.

Longevity: Good.

Faults: Include erect or partially erect ears.

The Komondor—the plural in Hungarian is *Komondorok*—is a large, white dog that looks like a dish-mop. It has been bred in its native Hungary for over 1000 years, and is one of the world's best guard dogs, bred to guard flocks and possessions. It will also protect your children and other livestock with its life. However, it does not take to strangers too kindly and is best in a country environment. Also, while it will live happily indoors, it is ideally suited to an outdoor kennel, its corded coat rendering it impervious to the cold.

Dogs average 31½in (80cm) high, bitches average 27½in (70cm). The color is always white. Ideally the skin is gray, but pink skin is acceptable.

The Old English Sheepdog

KEY FACTS

Character: Great stamina and sound temperament. Gets on well with children and other animals.

Exercise: Plenty. A good, big yard is essential for this boisterous breed.

Grooming: Daily brushing. Comb with steel comb. Lengthy show preparation.

Feeding: Approximately 2½ cans (14oz/400g size) of a branded meaty product, with biscuit added in equal part by volume.

Longevity: Average.

Faults: Include light eyes.

Varieties: From left to right: gray, grizzle, and blue.

"Bobtail," or the Old English Sheepdog, is thought to have resulted from the crossing of the Briard with the large Russian Owtscharka, which is related to Hungarian Sheepdogs. It was once used in England as cattle dog and guard. Nowadays it is kept almost solely as a family pet, and while it is a good-natured dog, it is not always a sensible choice for the suburban home because of its sheer bulk and exuberance.

Indeed, over-popularity in Britain following the breed's appearance in a television commercial has resulted in rescue societies being inundated with requests from owners wanting a home found for "Bobtails" which they bought on impulse and found too large to cope with in an apartment, or to exercise alongside a stroller. But in the right environment it is a first-rate companion, devoted and sensible and good with children.

Standing 24in (61cm) or more, bitches 22in (56cm) or more, the "Bobtail" comes in any shade of gray, grizzle, or blue. Body and hindquarters have solid color with or without white socks.

The Welsh Corgi

Pembroke varieties: From left to right: sable, black and tan, red, and fawn.

Welsh Corgi (Pembroke)

The Welsh Corgi (Cardigan) is one of Britain's most ancient breeds, brought over from the continent by the Celts more than 3,000 years ago. It is thought to originate from the same stock as the German Basset Hound. It has worked in Wales since the 11th century and is mentioned in Domesday Book, which was instigated by William the Conqueror. Its traditional role was always to move cattle by nipping at their ankles, a habit for which it is famous, as the servants and staff of Queen Elizabeth II know to their cost.

The Welsh Corgi (Pembroke) came over in the company of Flemish weavers who were summoned by Henry I in 1107 to introduce their craft into Wales. The Pembroke is related to various Nordic dogs such as the Samoyed and Norwegian Elkhound.

The two Corgis only began to resemble each other in the middle of the 19th century when the two types were crossed. The Pembroke is taller and shorter in the body than the Cardigan, which is instantly recognizable by its foxy tail.

The Welsh Corgi Cardigan stands 12in (30cm) at the shoulder and may be any color, with or without white markings. White should not predominate.

The Welsh Corgi Pembroke stands 10–12in (25.4–30.5cm) at the shoulder. Colors are self in red, sable, fawn, black-and-tan with or without white markings on legs, brisket, and neck. Some white on head and foreface is allowed.

A word of warning: don't allow your pet Corgi to jump on and off chairs if it is overweight, or this could result in back problems.

A popular pet, the Corgi is also a great favorite with the show ring fraternity.

KEY FACTS

Character: Devoted companion, tireless worker, and fine guard.

Exercise: Despite its traditional role as a worker, will settle for regular walks. Don't neglect these or the Corgi will lose its waistline.

Grooming: Daily brushing is all that is needed for this breed's water-resistant coat.

Feeding: Approximately ¾ can (14oz/400g size) of a branded meaty product, with biscuit added in equal part by volume.

Longevity: Good to average.

Faults: Inherent tendency to nip. The Cardigan has the slightly quieter temperament.

Cardigan varieties: From left to right: fawn and white, black and white, red and white, sable, tan, brown, and black.

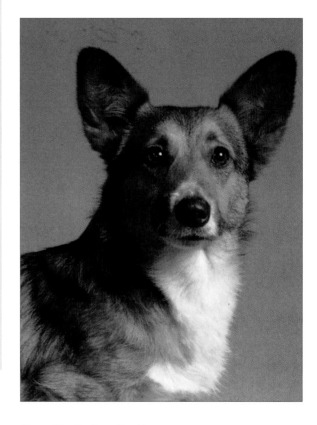

Above: The Cardigan Corgi is a very ancient breed that originated in Europe. In the past it was used as a cattle dog. This type of coat is known as blue merle—a mixture of gray, black, and blue hair.

Left: The Pembroke Corgi is longer in the leg and shorter in the body than the Cardigan. The two Corgis were recognized as separate breeds in Britain in 1934.

The German Shepherd

Varieties: From left to right: black and gold, black, gray, black and tan, and white.

One of the most popular dogs in the world, the German Shepherd has been attributed to the Bronze Age wolf, and, indeed, around the 7th century AD, a sheepdog of this type, but with a lighter coat, existed in Germany. By the 16th century the coat had darkened.

First exhibited in Hanover in 1882, the German Shepherd was introduced into the United Kingdom after the First World War by a band of dedicated fanciers who had seen the breed working in Germany. However, at that time it was considered inappropriate to glorify a breed with a Germanic name and it therefore became known not as the German Shepherd, but the Alsatian. It didn't revert to its original and correct name until 1971. There are many today who still refer to the breed as the Alsatian.

The German Shepherd is undoubtedly one of the most intelligent of breeds. It has fought valiantly in wars, been used as a guide dog for the blind,

police, and search and rescue dog, and successful obedience competitor.

LOVE AND TRAINING

Sadly, the reputation this breed has for ferocity is largely due to breed members falling into the wrong hands. The bored, restless, nervous German Shepherd can indeed be dangerous. However, the dog that is carefully trained, loved, and given a task to do which will satisfy its boundless energy and keen intelligence should have no problems.

The German Shepherd is a faithful defender of any children in the family, trouble only arising when, for example, it might misinterpret a move toward a child in its care.

The German Shepherd is constantly "on guard," noting any move on the part of a visitor which might constitute a threat to its beloved family.

Teaching this breed to be aggressive is sheer stupidity. The instinct to defend should the need arise is inbuilt.

Sadly, the GSD, as it is affectionately called, is subject to hip dysplasia—malformation of the ball of the hip joint, which can result in chronic lameness before middle age. Because of this, and the fact that the breed's great popularity has caused the commercially minded to breed from poor stock, it is all the more important to select a breeding kennel with great care.

Standing 25in (62.5cm) tall, bitches 23in (57.5cm), allowable colors are black or black saddle with tan, or gold to light gray markings. All-black, all-gray, or gray with lighter or brown markings are referred to as "sables." The white German Shepherd, although widely used by the armed forces, is not recognized by the American Kennel Club.

Above: The Groenendael is the most popular of the varieties of Belgian Shepherd Dog.

Below: The German Shepherd is a direct descendant of the wolf. It is constantly on the alert, ready to protect its family, and benefits from being given obedience or agility tasks to.perform to keep it occupied.

KEY FACTS

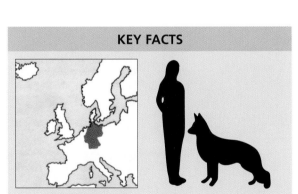

Character: Versatile and alert working dog with keen scenting ability. Excellent guard.

Exercise: Needs plenty. Best to channel its keen intelligence and exuberance into tasks such as obedience or agility.

Grooming: Daily brushing.

Feeding: 1½–2½ cans (14oz/400g size) of a branded meaty product, with biscuit added in equal part by volume.

Longevity: Good to average.

Faults: Include a possible tendency to overguard.

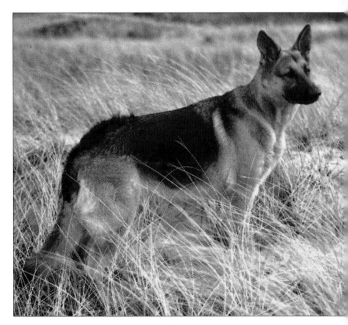

103

The Border Collie

The Border Collie (the term "Border" refers to the border country of England, Scotland, and Wales) has become almost a folk hero through its television appearances at sheepdog trials and obedience competitions. A hardy, working sheepdog, it is also the undoubted favorite of the obedience trainers and has, not all that wisely, been increasingly taken into suburban homes in the role of family pet. A natural herder (anything from pigs to people), the home is perhaps not the best environment for this worker which, while it has a fondness for children, can become bored and snappy through lack of exercise, freedom, and space.

The present-day Border Collies are a modern strain descended from collies of the lowland and border counties of England and Scotland. They are working sheepdogs of a distinct, recognizable type and have been exported, often at great cost, to many countries of the world.

The ideal height of the Border Collie is 21in (53cm), bitches slightly less, and a variety of colors is permissible, although white should never be the predominant color.

A young Border Collie will crouch instinctively in the presence of sheep. Farmers generally get an older working Collie to teach them their paces.

Above: The Smooth Collie, because of its lack of a thick coat, shows the athletic shape of the collies.

Varieties: A variety of markings is permissible, but white should never predominate.

KEY FACTS

Character: Tenacious, hardworking sheepdog of great tractability. Not suitable for suburban environment.
Exercise: Ample if it is not to become bored and snappy.
Grooming: Brush with an equine dandy brush. Remove dead fur after grooming.
Feeding: 1–1½ cans (14oz/400g size) of a branded meaty product, with biscuit added in equal part by volume.
Longevity: Good average.
Faults: Include any tendency to coarseness or weediness.

Below: The Rough Collie comes from the lowlands of Scotland, where it has a long history as a herding dog.

Below right: Another native of Scotland, the Bearded Collie is an intelligent and lively dog that loves plenty of exercise.

The Griffon

The Griffon comes in two varieties: the rough (Brussels Griffon) and the smooth, more correctly known as the Griffon Brabançon. In Britain the breed is referred to as the Griffon Bruxellois.

The Griffon is an affectionate, intelligent, happy little dog, with an almost human expression. It revels in being with its owner and will follow for miles, whether picking up driftwood on a beach, or walking sedately in the park. However, while they have the facility to follow, they are not the easiest of breeds to leash-train. Perseverance is the key.

Generally good natured with children and other pets, the Griffon is an excellent house dog, but does have the tendency to yap if unchecked. Like other short-nosed breeds, great care must be taken that it does not become overheated in warm weather, and that there is adequate ventilation and drinking water.

Whether to choose the rough- or smooth-coated variety is a matter of personal inclination. Roughs seem to come away with more prizes in the

Above: A Rough-coated Griffon, or Brussels Griffon. Black and tan is one of three color varieties. The Rough's coat needs regular attention.

KEY FACTS

Character: Hardy, happy, intelligent, and devoted.
Exercise: Adaptable. Not too keen on leash. Will follow for miles, or settle for a walk in the park.
Grooming: Rough coat needs stripping smooth coat needs brushing, toweling and rubbing down with chamois leather.
Feeding: Approximately ½ can (14oz/400g size) of a branded meaty product, with biscuit added in equal part by volume.
Longevity: Long lived.
Faults: Include high stepping front movement.

show ring, perhaps because of their sheer numbers, but their coats do need a fair amount of attention.

Sometimes referred to as "the mongrel of the purebred dog world" the Griffon is said to derive from the Affenpinscher, while the smooth-coat undoubtedly owes much to the Pug.

A ROYAL FAVORITE
Once used in stables to kill vermin, the Griffon was first exhibited at the Brussels Exhibition in 1880. Later

it found immense popularity when the much loved Queen Astrid of the Belgians took a fancy to the breed, though numbers were severely reduced during the war years (1940–45).

Today the Griffon is loved and exhibited in many countries of the world.

The Griffon weighs from 5–11lb (2.2–5kg), 6–10lb (2.7–4.5kg) most desirable, and comes in clear red, black, or black and rich tan, without white markings.

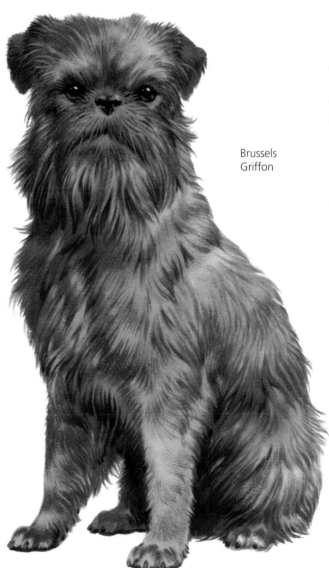

Brussels Griffon

Above: The smooth-coated, or Griffon Brabançon. Its face clearly shows its Pug ancestry.

Varieties: From left to right: black and tan, black, and red.

The Affenpinscher

This dog, with its monkey-like appearance, is well named. The Affenpinscher is a German breed, and the word *Affe* is German for "monkey." Indeed, the Germans often call this little dog the Zwergaffenpinscher —*Zwerg* meaning "dwarf"—while the French call it the "moustached devil." It is the smallest of the Schnauzers and Pinschers, but would do battle with a lion if roused!

Until 1896, miniature Pinschers and Affenpinschers were classified as one breed. In that year, however, it was decreed that the long-coats should thereafter be known as Affenpinschers and they were shown as such at the Berlin Show.

In fact the Affenpinscher has been in Germany at least since the Middle Ages, and is included in famous paintings by Jan van Eyck (1395–1441) and Albrecht Dürer (1471–1528). However, despite this strong Germanic connection, controversy exists as to whether, as is supposed, it contributed to the Griffon Bruxellois, or the other way around.

A comic, lovable little fellow with a mind of its own, the Affenpinscher, which is black, sometimes with gray shading, stands 9½–11in (24–28cm) tall and weighs 6½–9lb (3–4kg).

KEY FACTS

Character: Lively, loving and self-confident, Carries itself with comic seriousness.
Exercise: Adaptable to town or country. Enjoys a walk.
Grooming: Regular trimming, daily brushing.
Feeding: Approximately ½ can (14oz/400g size) of a branded meaty product, with biscuit added in equal part by volume.
Longevity: Good.
Faults: Include hackneyed action.

The Chinese Crested Dog

KEY FACTS

Character: Happy, never vicious, extremely energetic and affectionate.

Exercise: Enjoys a walk but tends to exercise itself rushing about in the home.

Grooming: Bathing about every three weeks, and skin treated with baby cream. Crest and tail plume brushed. Shave off any stray hairs for show.

Feeding: Rapacious appetite but averagely ½–¾ can (14oz/400g size) of a branded meaty product, with biscuit added in equal part by volume.

Longevity: Average.

Faults: Include light eyes. They should be so dark as to appear black.

Varieties: From top to bottom: brown-spotted, blue, black-spotted, silver gray.

The Chinese Crested Dog was almost extinct when, in 1966, Mrs. Ruth Harris of Gloucestershire in England contacted an elderly lady in the United States who owned the only remaining examples of the breed. Mrs. Harris imported several of these. The breed is kept both for the show ring and as household pets.

"POWDER PUFFS"

Happy and scatty, the Chinese Crested is an extremely active little dog which simply cannot resist the temptation to use a room as a race circuit. It is, however, lovable, reasonably intelligent, good-natured and usually fairly easy to train to the lead. Strange but true is that haired examples of the breed, known as Powder Puffs, appear in almost every litter, and are thought to be nature's way of keeping the other, hairless, pups warm.

The Chinese Crested comes in two distinct body types: the deer, which is racy and fine-boned, and the cobby, which is heavier in body and bone. It stands 11–13in (28–33cm) at the withers, bitches 9–12in (23–30cm). Weight should not be over 12lb (5.5kg).

109

The Yorkshire Terrier

So popular has the Yorkshire Terrier become that there are many specimens about in varying sizes. The unknowledgeable will tell you that their pet is, or isn't, a "miniature." In fact, the standard for the breed calls for a dog up to 7lb (3kg) in weight—that is only one pound more than the standard for the world's smallest dog, the Chihuahua. However, there is no doubt that some of the bigger Yorkies one sees around do make happy, hardy pets.

With its keen terrier temperament in a small frame, the Yorkie makes a first-rate companion, and will live happily whether in an apartment or on a farm. However, the show specimen tends to live a sedate life, spending most of its time done up in rag-like paper curlers.

KEY FACTS

Character: Alert, intelligent terrier in a small frame.
Exercise: Will walk its owner literally off his or her feet in the country, or settle for a walk in the park.
Grooming: Daily brushing and combing for the pet owner. Continuous work for the show aspirant.
Feeding: Approximately ½ can (14oz/400g size) of a branded meaty product, with biscuit added in equal part by volume.
Longevity: The 16-year-old Yorkie is not a rarity, but obviously there is no hard and fast rule.
Faults: Described as the tyrant of the dog world, it may well take you over, with your household, if unchecked.

The origin of this little dog is fairly new. Its ancestry traces back only about 100 years to the crossing of a Skye Terrier with the old Black and Tan Terrier. Rumor has it that the Maltese Terrier and even the Dandie Dinmont may also have, played a part.

The Yorkie, whose coat should hang quite straight and evenly down each side, with a parting extending from the nose to the end of the tail, should be dark steel blue in color (not silver blue), extending from the occiput to the roof of the tail, never mingled with fawn, bronze, or dark hairs. The hair on its chest should be a rich, bright tan, and all tan hair must be darker at the roots than in the middle, shading still lighter at the tips.

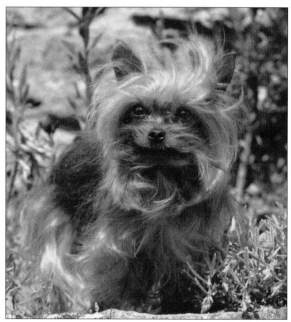

Above: The Maltese Terrier is one of the oldest dog breeds. Records of it go back at least to Roman times.

Right: The Yorkie's coat should be dark steel blue, with a rich tan color across the chest. It needs daily grooming to keep it looking its best.

111

The Pomeranian

KEY FACTS

Character: Happy, hardy, and devoted. Thinks it is a much bigger dog.

Exercise: Some Pomeranians are exercised in the garden or park, others go for long walks in the countryside with their owners.

Grooming: Plenty of time needed to care for the Pom's double coat—a short, fluffy under-coat and a long, straight top coat. Daily brushing with stiff brush. Regular trimming.

Feeding: Approximately ½ can (14oz/400g size) of a branded meaty product, with biscuit added in equal part by volume.

Longevity: Many live into their teens.

Faults: Include eyes set too wide apart.

The Pomeranian, with its foxy head and intelligent expression, comes in a whole variety of colors, but must be free from black or white shadings. Whole colors are white, black, brown, light or dark blue (as pale as possible), orange (as self-colored and bright as possible), beaver, and cream. Creams have black noses and black eye-rims. Whites must be quite free from lemon or any other color.

Varieties: From top to bottom: White, brown, orange, blue, beaver, black and cream.

The Pomeranian, once Queen Victoria's favorite until ousted by the Imperial Pekingese, is often wrongly thought of as the lap dog of elderly ladies. It lends itself well to that role, but is well equipped to tackle a country walk with its owner.

The breed, which is thought to be of European origin, takes its name from Pomerania. However, being a small Spitz it is more than likely that its beginnings were in the Arctic Circle. It was, in any case, a much larger dog, up to 30lb (3.6kg) in weight before being bred down, until in 1896 shows were divided into classes for Poms over and under that weight. Since 1915, the over 8lb (3.6kg) variety has been eliminated.

The Miniature Pinscher

KEY FACTS

Character: Fearless, self-possessed, and spirited. Intelligent and easy to look after.
Exercise: Suitable for town and country and will adapt to its owner's needs.
Grooming: Daily brush and rub-down with a chamois leather.
Feeding: Approximately ½ can (14oz/400g size) of a branded meaty product. with biscuit added in equal part by volume.
Longevity: Good to average.
Faults: Include hocks which turn in or out.

Varieties From top to bottom: black, fawn, blue, and chocolate and tan.

The delightful Miniature Pinscher (commonly known as the "Min Pin") is not, as many suppose, a bred-down version of the Doberman. It is a much older breed, a descendant of the German Smooth-haired Pinscher to which the Dachshund and Italian Hound probably contributed.

The Min Pin is a high-stepping little dog, a natural showman, and a joy to watch. It has, however, got a mind of its own and, in common with many small breeds, is likely to yap if unchecked. It is so attractive that most owners let their Min Pins get away with murder.

Standing from 10–12in (25.5–30cm) at the withers, the Miniature Pinscher may be black, blue, chocolate with sharply defined tan markings, or solid red.

It did, incidentally, receive purebred (Pedigree) status in 1895 from the German Pinscher-Schnauzer Klub.

113

The Pekingese

The Pekingese always seems aware of its regal background. In fact, it came to the West after 1860, when British troops looted and burned the Summer Palace at Peking. Five Pekingese were found in the women's apartments and taken back to England. Nicknamed "Looty," one was presented to Queen Victoria and became a great favorite, later being painted by the artist Landseer.

DEVOTED DOGS

The Peke may not receive the same devotion as when slave girls in the imperial palace were used as wet nurses to suckle them and eunuchs employed to watch over them, but they still manage to have their every whim catered for and are extremely forceful characters whose affection has to be earned by its owner. Once given, one could not wish for a more devoted companion.

Below: The Tibetan Spaniel is probably descended from the Lhaso Apso and Chinese Spaniels. It was considered to be sacred and led a carefully guarded life in palaces and monasteries.

KEY FACTS

Character: Aloof, dignified, small, well-balanced dog of quality.

Exercise: Despite its glamorous appearance in the show ring, the Pekingese enjoys nothing better than a good long scamper in the mud. Park walks will suffice.

Grooming: Daily brushing with a soft-bristled brush. Best to tackle the underside with the Peke lying on its back.

Feeding Approximately ½ can (14oz/400g size) of a branded meaty product, with biscuit added in equal part by volume.

Longevity: Can live well into the teens.

Faults: Include domed skull.

This is not a kennel dog, but a companion which appreciates the freedom of the house.

The ideal weight for the Pekingese should not exceed 11lb (5kg), bitches 12lb (5.5kg). There are also what are known as "sleeve" Pekes (so named, it is believed, because they were concealed in the large sleeves of the mandarins' gowns), which weigh no more than 6lb (2.75kg). The breed comes in various acceptable colors and markings, except for the outlawed albino or liver. Parti-colors should be evenly broken.

Above: The Japanese Chin probably descends mainly from the Pekinese and the Tibetan Spaniel. It first arrived in Europe during the 15ᵗʰ century.

Varieties: From left to right: sable biscuit and white, black and tan, brown and white, red, white, brown, and black.

The Cavalier King Charles Spaniel

A larger toy breed, the Cavalier is immensely popular because of its good temperament and attractive appearance. It is a faithful, loving companion, reliable with children, and draws enormous entries in dog show classes.

Cavalier King Charles Spaniel

Alas, there must be many who set out to get either a Cavalier or a King Charles Spaniel and come home with the other simply because they do not know the difference. In fact, the Cavalier is larger and, unlike the King Charles's well-domed skull, the Cavalier's is almost flat between the ears, and its stop is much shallower. It is a matter of choice, for they both share the same characteristics.

The Cavalier and the King Charles both trace back to common stock. The King Charles can trace its ancestry to Japan 2,000 years ago, and became popular at the Stuart court in 16th-century England. It has often been related how King Charles II of England spent more time playing with his spaniels in council chambers than attending to affairs of state and how he would take his pets into the bedchamber.

In fact, the King Charles was more like the Cavalier, having a longer nose. It was when shorter nosed dogs became fashionable that the King Charles as we know it came about, the old type almost disappearing, until in the late 1920s a group of devotees determined to bring back the older type—which they wisely prefixed with the word "Cavalier."

The Cavalier weighs 12–18lb (5.4–8kg) and comes in a number of attractive colors: black and tan, ruby (entirely colored rich red), Blenheim (rich chestnut markings, well broken up, on a pearly white ground) and tricolor (black-and-white, well spaced).

Varieties: From left to right: Blenheim, ruby, tricolor, and black and tan.

KEY FACTS

Character: Sporting, affectionate, and fearless.

Exercise: Should not be kenneled out of doors, but the Cavalier enjoys a good walk with its owner.

Grooming: Daily brushing with bristle brush. Eyes should be kept clear of tear streaks.

Feeding: Approximately ¾ can (14oz/400g size) of a branded meaty product, with biscuit added in equal part by volume.

Longevity: Good.

Faults: Include possible over-popularity, resulting in some poor stock—so choose your breeder with care.

Above left: The Cavalier King Charles has a flattish head between the ears, and comes in a variety of colors, including Blenheim (chestnut and white), shown here.

Left: The King Charles Spaniel has a high-domed head and very long ears.

117

The Chihuahua

Left: The long-coated Chihuahua. Despite their small size, Chihuahuas are very intelligent and brave.

The Chihuahua is the smallest dog in the world, its ideal weight being 2–6lb (0.9–2.7kg), but there are many specimens below or above the standard weight which make good pets. Whatever their weight, Chihuahuas do not consider themselves small dogs. They think they are enormous, and are foolhardy enough to take on all comers. It is typical of a Chihuahua to race up and growl, for instance, at a Doberman which, if it is lucky, will treat it with disdain.

Although it will get on with other pets, the Chihuahua much prefers to be with its own kind. It adores its owner, although the pup or newcomer will take a little time to give its wholehearted trust, and is determined from the outset to become the VIP member of the household. It may be small, but it is supremely intelligent.

The Chihuahua is called after the Mexican state of that name, and is reputed to have been the sacred dog of the Incas. From the evidence it is probable that the hairless dogs which came to South America from China had a part in producing the delightful Chihuahua.

Below: The Papillon, so-called for its wing-shaped ears. Its origins are unclear, but it may be descended in part from the Chihuahua. It was a very fashionable breed in Europe.

KEY FACTS

Character: Devoted, clannish, keenly intelligent. Splendid miniature guard.

Exercise: Don't be misled into thinking that Chihuahuas are just for carrying. They can be, but you would be surprised how much they enjoy a good walk.

Grooming: Brush with a soft brush and rub down with a velvet pad or chamois leather to make the coat gleam. Don't neglect tear stains around eyes.

Feeding: ⅓–½ can (14oz/400g size) of a branded meaty product, with biscuit added in equal part by volume.

Longevity: Can live well into the teens, but the particularly tiny specimens rarely do so.

Faults: Include tipped or broken-down ears.

SMOOTH AND LONG COATS

Chihuahuas come with both smooth and long coats, and which you choose is a matter of preference. Some people like smooth-coated dogs, others like the glamor of a long coat, or simply enjoy having a luxuriant coat to brush. At one time, the two types were allowed to interbreed, so that one might have both smooth and long coats in the same litter, but this is no longer permissible and there are separate show classes for the two varieties. The long-coats are currently more popular.

The Chihuahua comes in any color or mixture of colors, including blue and chocolate. Eyes are dark or, in the case of the chocolate, ruby. Light eyes in light colors are allowed.

Varieties: Top from left to right: cream, fawn, black and white; bottom from left to right: brown and tan, brown and white, and black and tan.

The Italian Grayhound

The graceful Italian Grayhound is a grayhound in miniature, but more slender in all proportions. It is a very loving, sensitive house-pet which nonetheless enjoys plenty of exercise. However, it is frightening that it was recently publicized as the "ideal pet": remember that it is a pet for extra-careful people who understand that clumsiness could lead to broken legs, that the little Italian feels the cold and always needs a coat in chill weather, and that harsh words cause this dainty pet very much pain.

An obvious descendant of the Grayhound, it has been around in its present form for a very long time. At one time there were disastrous attempts to miniaturize the breed further with an infusion of English Toy Terrier blood and it was not until the early 1970s, following the import from Italy of fresh stock, that the breed really got on its feet again.

This keen little rabbiter weighs only 6–10lb (2.7–4.5kg) and comes in black, blue, cream, fawn, red, or white, or any of these colors broken with white.

KEY FACTS

Character: Intelligent, graceful, gentle, and obedient.
Exercise: Enjoys plenty of freedom. But beware, those slender legs break easily.
Grooming: Brush and rub down with chamois leather.
Feeding: Approximately ½ can (14oz/400g size) of a branded meaty product, with biscuit added in equal part by volume.
Longevity: Good average.
Faults: Include black or blue dogs with tan markings—or, especially, brindled.

Varieties: From left to right: fawn, black and white, white, cream, black, red, and blue.

Below: The Whippet is descended from the Italian Grayhound crossed with terrier blood. It was first bred in the 19th century in the north of England, for hare coursing.

The Airedale Terrier

Right: Although a typical terrier, the Welsh terrier adapts well to family life.

Below right: The Lakeland Terrier is related to the Welsh Terrier, which shares common ancestors with the Airedale.

KEY FACTS

Character: Friendly, courageous, and intelligent. Good with children.

Exercise: Needs plenty, particularly if kept in town.

Grooming: Daily brushing with a stiff brush. Professional stripping twice a year.

Feeding: Approximately 1–1½ cans (14oz/400g size) of a branded meaty product, with biscuit added in equal part by volume.

Longevity: Good average.

Faults: Include pendulous ears, or ears set too high.

The Airedale is the largest of the terriers and is what could be described as a "True Brit", named after its place of origin in the Aire Valley (Dale) of Yorkshire. Yorkshire gamekeepers kept terriers to control vermin and these were undoubtedly crossed with the Otterhound to produce the Airedale. It is an excellent ratter, ducker, and can even be trained to the gun and, of course, for obedience.

The Airedale has a steady temperament, likes to be part of the family and makes a splendid playmate for children. However, while some Airedales are docile as lambs there are those which are not averse to a good scrap with other dogs, chasing motorbikes, and making something of a nuisance of themselves. So it is vitally important to buy a pup from a kennel which breeds for both quality and temperament. A good Airedale is a joy and a pleasure to behold. However, the show Airedale does have to be hand-stripped, an art which must be learnt by the owner if a certain amount of expense is not to be incurred.

Incidentally, the Airedale worked as a police dog before the German Shepherd largely took over that role. It has also been a patrol dog for the dock and railway police and served in the armed forces.

Despite its size, 23–24in (58–61cm), bitches 22–23in (56–59cm), the Airedale is a dog that can live happily in town, provided that it receives sufficient exercise.

Colors are body-saddle black or grizzle at the top of the neck and top surface of tail, all other parts tan.

Varieties: From top to bottom: black and tan, and grizzle.

The Norfolk Terrier

The Norfolk and Norwich Terriers are practically identical except for their ears: the Norfolk's are lop, the Norwich's prick. The Norfolk also has a slightly longer neck. A useful trick used by the British for identifying the breeds is to recall that the Norfolk's ears are flat like the county of that name, and that the ears of the Norwich stand up like the towers of Norwich Cathedral!

The Norwiches and Norfolks were developed in England in the 1880s. Earlier, in the 1860s, a Colonel Vaughan of Ballybrick in Ireland had hunted with a pack of small red terriers evolved from the Irish terrier from which the many resulting out-crossed prick-eared and drop-eared terriers came about. At one time the ears of the drop-eared terriers were cropped, but following an outcry the practice became illegal.

Also credited with the evolution of the Norwich is Jodrell Hopkins, a horse dealer from Trumpington,

Below: The Border Terrier came from the England–Scottish border. It is a good hunter, hardy and fast, and has been used to improve other breeds.

KEY FACTS

Character: Lovable, hardy, and active. Good family pet.

Exercise: Like most terriers. these little dogs like nothing better than a good scamper in the country, but will adapt to town life.

Grooming: Routine brushing and combing. Some trimming.

Feeding: ½–1 can (14oz/400g size) of a branded meaty product, with biscuit added in equal part by volume.

Longevity: Good lifespan.

Faults: Include tendency to chase small livestock, if unchecked. (They love farm life and can be taught to guard rather than chase stock.)

Cambridge. Mr. Hopkins owned a bitch, some of the pups of which were acquired by his employee, Frank Jones. Jones crossed them with other terriers, including the Glen of Imaal Terrier, and called the progeny "Jones" or "Trumpington" terriers. These dogs were particularly popular with the undergraduates at Cambridge University who called them "Jones terriers" and it was not until after World War I that the name Norwich terrier came into use.

In 1964 the Norwich and the Norfolk terriers were recognized as one breed by the United Kingdom's Kennel Club, and in January 1979 the two dogs were awarded separate status. Hardy and good with children, the Norfolks make ideal pets.

The Norfolk and the Norwich stand 10in (25–26cm) and come in all shades of red, wheaten, black and tan, tall or grizzle. White marks or patches are disliked by show judges.

Norfolk Terrier

Right: The Norwich Terrier, which differs from the Norfolk only in its prick ears.

Varieties: From top to bottom: wheaten, red, grizzle, and black and tan.

The Bull Terrier

As with most bull breeds, people seem either to love them or hate them. There are those who consider the Bull Terrier the ugliest creature imaginable; others who find them tremendously appealing. They were bred for fighting and the instinct is still strong enough for them to take on all comers—and win. Therefore, they are not really a dog for the beginner. However, let it be said that they make devoted and loyal pets, are sound with children (particularly the bitch), and that, provided they are firmly but kindly disciplined, and kept in the right environment—not an apartment—the owner should have no problems.

Bull Terrier

When bull baiting was outlawed by Parliament in 1835, a band of fanciers (including James Hinks of Birmingham, England) was determined to maintain the breed and improve it, while retaining its great strength and tenacity. This was achieved by crossing the White English Terrier with the Bulldog and the Dalmatian, thereby producing a new breed of English Bull Terrier. It was only later that the Brindle Bull Terrier came on the scene.

The Bull Terrier has no official height or weight limit, but its standard calls for maximum substance for size of dog consistent with quality and sex.

Colors are white, black, brindle, red, fawn, and tricolor.

Left: There is no official size range for the Bull Terrier. The example illustrated is a Miniature.

Below: The Bull Terrier comes in a number of colors, including white.

KEY FACTS

Character: Described as the gladiator of the canine race.
Exercise: Active dog that needs a great deal of exercise.
Grooming: Brushing and rub-down will keep the coat in good condition.
Feeding: Approximately 1½ cans (14oz/400g size) of a branded meaty product, with biscuit added in equal part by volume.
Longevity: Average.
Faults: Include obstinacy, and blue or partly blue eyes.

Varieties: Top from left to right: white and black; middle from left to right: red and fawn; bottom from left to right: brindle and tricolor.

127

The Staffordshire Bull Terrier

The popular "Staffy" certainly makes a devoted household pet that can be trusted with children. It cannot, however, always be trusted with other dogs and you may sometimes find it an embarrassment to be on the end of the lead of a pet which is straining to "have a go" at its fellows. A good idea is to take it to a dog training class when it is a pup so that it becomes accustomed to other dogs.

The Staffordshire Bull Terrier is the product of a Bulldog and terrier mating in the 19th century. It is thought that the Bulldog's partner might well have been the Old English Black-and-Tan Terrier which preceded the Manchester Terrier, a breed which has been recognized by the United Kingdom Kennel Club since the 1930s.

Above: The Bulldog was one of the partners mated to breed the Staffordshire Bull Terrier during the 19th century. Its contribution of short legs, deep chest, and an amiable disposition toward humans have helped the "Staffy" gain a devoted following.

KEY FACTS

Character: Courageous, intelligent, affectionate. Super pet, wonderful with children, but has a liking for fights with other dogs.

Exercise: Boundless energy. Like the Bull Terrier, best in a controlled country situation.

Grooming A brush and rub down will keep the coat gleaming.

Feeding: 1–1½ cans (14oz/400g size) of a branded meaty product, with biscuit added in equal part by volume.

Longevity: Good to average.

Faults: Include full, drop, or pricked ears.

AMERICAN STAFFORDSHIRE TERRIER

The "Staffy" is not the same as the infamous Pit Bull Terrier, the correct name for which is the American Staffordshire Terrier. (At one time the American Kennel Club did allow the American "Staffy" to be shown with the Staffordshire Bull Terrier, and crossbreeding of the two was permitted.) The Pit Bull was evolved in England from the mating of an English Bulldog and an English terrier, the result being a much heavier dog altogether than the Staffordshire Bull. Once it had reached the United States in 1870 it soon became known as the Pit Dog, Pit Bull Terrier and Yankee Terrier. Pit Bulls are not recommended as pets.

The Staffordshire Bull Terrier weighs 28–38lb (13–17kg), bitches 24–34lb (11–15.5kg), and stands 11–15.5cm (14–16in) high; these heights being related to the weights. Colors are red, fawn, white, black, or blue, or any one of these colors with white; and any shade of brindle or of brindle with white. Don't buy a "Staffy" that is black-and-tan or liver color if you intend to exhibit in the show ring, for those colors are considered undesirable.

Varieties: From top to bottom: fawn, white, red, black, blue, brindle, and red and while.

The West Highland White Terrier

The popular "Westie" is a true Scot, sharing common ancestry with the Dandie Dinmont and Cairn Terriers. In the early 1900s many such terriers, which were bred to hunt vermin and other small animals, were banded together, but we do know that in the late 19th century a Colonel Malcolm of Poltalloch had a strain of white Scottish terriers, known as Poltalloch or Roseneath Terriers.

An adaptable, happy pet that will live indoors or in an outside kennel—but infinitely prefers to share the fireside—the "Westie" has become immensely popular and there are many poor specimens about, so

it is well worth seeking out a good breeder if you are thinking of acquiring one.

Standing approximately 11in (28cm) high at the withers, and weighing 15–18lb (7–8.5kg) the West Highland White Terrier comes in one color only, white, so don't, as so many people do, mix him up with the black Scottish Terrier (the "Scottie"), once known as the Aberdeen Terrier. The West Highland White Terrier is also shorter in the back, and has a shorter head and smaller ears, than the Scottie. Its eyes should be dark and widely set and its ears small and pointed.

KEY FACTS

Character: Game, hardy, adaptable, and attractive pet that gets on with children and other pets.

Exercise: A born ratter and hunter, this keen terrier will adapt to suburban living, but do ensure that it gets the exercise it deserves.

Grooming: Daily brushing and combing. However, like the Airedale, needs twice-yearly hand stripping and constant work on its coat it you aspire to the show ring.

Feeding: Approximately 1 can (14oz/400g size) of a branded meaty product, with biscuit added in equal part by volume.

Longevity: Good.

Faults: Include a nose that projects forward, and light colored eyes.

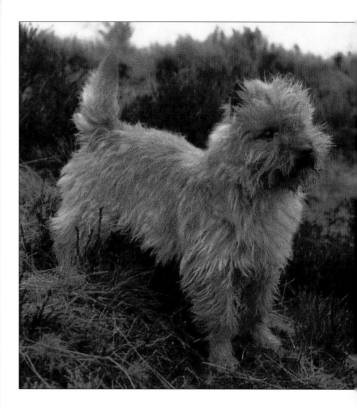

Above: The Cairn Terrier shares a common ancestry with the West Highland. It was not until the 20th century that these small terrier breeds were distinguished from one another.

Below : The Dandie Dinmont, originating from the English–Scottish border, is also related to the Cairn.

The Setters

Below: The Gordon Setter is black with tan markings. Its ancestry probably includes Bloodhound and Collie blood.

Confusion sometimes exists as to which setter is which. In fact, the Irish (or Red) Setter is the most popular and, if one is frank, the most scatty, especially in youth. It is ideal as a family pet, as a gundog, or in stables, where it can run with the horses. It evolved from crossing Irish Water Spaniels, Springer Spaniels, English and Gordon Setters and the Spanish Pointer. The Irish Setter began life as a red-and-white dog and, indeed, Irish Red and White Setters are now making their mark as a separate breed.

The English Setter, again good with children and a first-class gundog, has distinctive black-and-white, lemon-and-white, liver-and-white or tricolor markings, and is reckoned to have evolved from spaniels, while the Gordon Setter, which is coal-black with tan markings (described as the color of a ripe horse-chestnut) is the only native Scottish gundog, bred at Gordon Castle, Banffshire, the seat of the Dukes of

Varieties: Left from top to bottom: black and white, liver and white, lemon and white, and tricolor; right from top to bottom: Irish (red), red and white, Gordon.

Setters are superb gundogs and make ideal pets. They are not by any manner of means guard dogs, and would be more likely to persuade a burglar to come and play than repel his entry!

KEY FACTS

Character: Beautiful, untiring, ready to hunt. Good with children, horses, and other animals.

Exercise: An exuberant animal which it would be cruel to keep in a confined environment.

Grooming: Daily grooming with a stiff brush. You will also need a steel comb to avoid tangles. Ask the breeder about trimming.

Feeding: At least 1½ cans (14oz/400g size) of a branded meaty product, with biscuit added in equal part by volume.

Longevity: Can live into the teens.

Faults: Include over-exuberance (should you consider that a fault).

Richmond and Gordon and originally known as the Gordon Castle Setter. The Collie and Bloodhound are attributed in its makeup.

Not so frequently seen as the Irish and English varieties, the Gordon has possibly the steadiest temperament of the three, being easy-going, calm, and docile. It is also a methodical hunter.

Setters stand about 25½–27in (65–68cm) high, bitches 24–25½in (61–65cm) and, in common with the Labrador and Golden Retriever, are an ideal choice for the family wishing to combine a good gundog with a first-class family pet. However, they need plenty of freedom, and do not take to being confined in a small area.

Above: The English Setter is probably descended from the spaniels. Black and white markings are one of a variety of colors acceptable in this breed.

Irish Red Setter

The Weimaraner

KEY FACTS

Character: Good temperament and stamina. Excels at obedience and agility.
Exercise: An exuberant dog that needs plenty of exercise and an outlet for keen intelligence.
Grooming: Daily brushing.
Feeding: 1½–2½ cans (14oz/400g size) of a branded meaty product, with biscuit added in equal part by volume.
Longevity: Good to average.
Faults: Include a tendency towards aggressiveness in some animals.

Varieties: From top to bottom: mouse gray, silver gray, and roe gray.

Below: The Hungarian Viszla is a breed with exceptional tracking and retrieving qualities, and it also makes a good family pet. Its ancestry dates back to the Middle Ages.

Nicknamed "The Silver Ghost," the Weimaraner has been both police dog and guard dog. It was, in fact, purpose bred as a gundog at the Weimar court in Germany in the late 18th century the defunct St. Hubert Hounds, Bloodhounds, and Pointers having a hand in its makeup. Since the early 1950s it has gained tremendous popularity in both Britain and America, where breed members have shone in the show ring both in beauty and obedience classes. The Weimaraner has also been widely sought after as a family pet, but here problems can arise for, although it is an affectionate animal, it is really not a beginner's dog and without proper training will assume control. It can live in town provided it receives sufficient exercise, but is certainly best when its keen intelligence has some satisfying task to keep it occupied.

The Weimaraner is a good-sized dog standing 24–27in (61–69cm) at the withers, bitches 22–25in (56–64cm), and is generally—and preferably—a distinctive silver-gray in color, though shades of mouse or roe gray are permissible, blending to a lighter shade on head and ears. Sometimes a dark "eel" stripe appears along the back.

Above: The Weimaraner has a good temperament, but is highly intelligent and needs expert training.

135

The Water Spaniel

An enchanting-looking animal, the Irish Water Spaniel is a first-class water dog skilled at wildfowling and trainable as an all-round gundog. It does however need obedience training from an early age and to be taught to get on with other animals. Nonetheless, it is affectionate and makes a good pet. It is also a better watchdog than most gundogs.

Like the standard Poodle, which also began life as a water retriever, the Irish Water Spaniel evolved in Ireland from several spaniel breeds toward the latter part of the 19th century.

The American Water Spaniel, which is frankly more spaniel-like in appearance, but has the same qualities as the Irish, is believed to have evolved from the crossing of the Irish Water Spaniel with, as would appear likely, a smaller spaniel or with the Curly Coated Retriever. It is sometimes called the Boykin Spaniel after one of the pioneers of the breed.

The Irish Water Spaniel stands 21–23in (53–58cm) high, bitches 20–22in (51–56cm) and has one color only: rich, dark liver with a purplish tint or bloom that is peculiar to the breed and is sometimes referred to as puce-liver.

The American Water Spaniel stands 15–18in (38–46cm) and may be solid liver in color or dark chocolate, possibly with white on the toes or chest.

Varieties: From left to right: liver and chocolate.

Irish Water Spaniel

KEY FACTS

Character: Devotion, endurance; first-class water dog. Good pet, but can be tricky with strangers.

Exercise: Needs plenty. Not an ideal choice for an enclosed environment.

Grooming: Regular brushing. Neglect this and its coat will mat. Some stripping.

Feeding: Approximately 1–1½ cans (14oz/400g size) of a branded meaty product, with biscuit added in equal part by volume.

Longevity: Good.

Faults: Include tendency to fight other dogs.

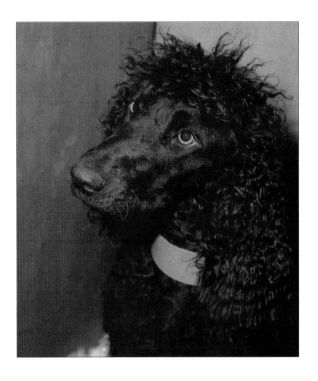

Above: The Irish Water Spaniel is dark liver in color. Its curly coat needs regular attention.

Left: Although classed as a separate breed, the only obvious difference between the curly-coated and flat-coated retrievers is their coats. The curly-coated is also a slightly heavier build.

The Golden Retriever

The beautiful Golden Retriever is kindly and trustworthy with children. It may be kenneled outdoors, but infinitely prefers to be inside as one of the family. Like the Labrador Retriever, it is a good all-purpose dog which ideally combines the role of owner's gundog with family pet. It works well in obedience and, being easy to train, is popular as a guide dog for the blind.

It is generally accepted that the Golden Retriever evolved from a litter of Retriever-cross Spaniel pups born on Lord Tweedmouth's Scottish estate in 1860. However, the rumor persists that their true ancestry sprang from a troupe of performing Russian Shepherd Dogs which his lordship saw performing in a circus at Brighton, Sussex. The story goes that, so impressed was Lord Tweedmouth with the dogs, he purchased the entire troupe, subsequently adding Bloodhound blood to improve the "nose."

The Golden Retriever stands 22–24in (56–61cm) at the withers, bitches 20–22in (51–56cm), and comes in any shade of gold or cream. A few white hairs, on the chest only are permissible.

Above: The Chesapeake Bay Retriever is thought to be descended from flat- and curly-coated Retrievers and Newfoundlands. It has webbed feet and a thick, oily coat, and is an excellent swimmer.

Varieties: From left to right: light gold, cream, and dark gold.

KEY FACTS

Character: Kindly expression with temperament to match. Good all-purpose gundog and family pet.

Exercise: Plenty of exercise to keep this dog fit, happy and in good shape.

Grooming: Regular brushing.

Feeding: At least 1½ cans (14oz/400g size) of a branded meaty product, with biscuit added in equal part by volume.

Longevity: Good to average.

Faults: Cowhocks are highly undesirable.

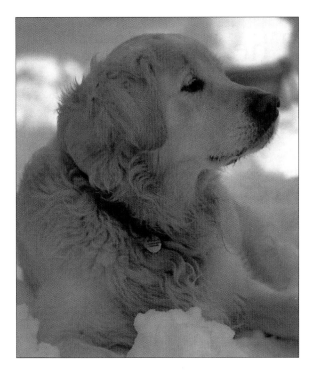

Above: The Golden Retriever combines the qualities of gundog and family pet.

The Labrador Retriever

Varieties: From left to right: black, yellow, and liver/chocolate.

KEY FACTS

Character: Good tempered, excellent companion, and fine gundog. Adaptable, devoted, and kind with children.
Exercise: Needs plenty. Has tendency to put on weight if given insufficient exercise, or overfed.
Grooming: Regular brushing.
Feeding: 1½–2½ cans (14oz/400g size) of a branded meaty product, with biscuit added in equal part by volume.
Longevity: Good average.
Faults: Cowhocks are highly undesirable.

The Labrador Retriever is often mistaken for the Golden Retriever. It is a natural mistake for both are retrievers of similar color. However, the Labrador has a short, dense coat without wave or feathering, unlike the Golden Retriever, which has a flat or wavy coat with good feathering. Think in terms of "Golden long" and "Labrador flat."

The Labrador is an extraordinarily popular dog, and justifiably so, for it is an excellent gundog that makes a fine family pet. It is somewhat

Labrador Retriever

exuberant in adolescence, but soon settles down and is extremely adaptable. However, it is important that it receives sufficient exercise. There are an awful lot of overweight Labradors around—particularly spayed bitches that are overfed and taken out for exercise too seldom.

FISHERMAN'S FRIEND

The Labrador Retriever comes from Newfoundland, where its original task was to help land the nets of fishermen, and its ability to swim survives. It has certainly existed in its present form since the 1830s, if not well before. Its present-day roles include police work, sniffing out drugs and explosives, and acting as a guide dogs for the blind.

The Labrador Retriever stands 22–22½in (56–57cm) high, bitches 21½in (54–56cm), and may be wholly black, yellow, or liver/chocolate. Yellows range from light cream to red fox. Blacks and yellows are most popular; yellows being more plentiful nowadays than the blacks, which some say are the better gundogs.

Below: The flat-coated Retriever can be distinguished by its longer coat, which is often wavy, and the feathering on its legs and tail.

Right: The Labrador Retriever has a flat, dense coat. It is most commonly either yellow or black, but chocolate brown occurs as well.

The Cocker Spaniel

Villar, an authority on the Cocker Spaniel, once wrote this sensible appraisal: "There is no more pleasant dog, nor one more affectionate and lively than the Cocker. His well developed psychology makes him extremely interesting. The qualities of intelligence, goodness, and cunning are all tied up together within him. He obeys not through servility but by sharing ideas with his master, whose slightest intention he is able to guess. He is most faithful, and also an excellent guard dog, wary of any suspicious sound and, if necessary, confronts an intruder with courage."

The Cocker, known in the United States as the English Cocker, in fact originated in Spain and can trace its ancestry back at least to the 14th century. It has been used in falconry and, while its task is generally to flush out game, it will also retrieve. It is a gentle, family dog and debatably one of the most beautiful in puppyhood. It responds to firm but kind training from an early age, and is an enthusiastic worker. There were some temperament problems with the goldens a few years ago, but hopefully these have now been eradicated.

KEY FACTS

Character: The "Merry Cocker" has an ever-wagging tail, is beautiful, intelligent, obedient, and a first-class family pet.
Exercise: Originally bred for hunting, the Cocker needs and enjoys plenty of exercise, particularly as, with its love of food, it can be in danger of losing its waistline.
Grooming: Daily brushing and combing to avoid tangles. Mind those ears don't drop into the food bowl and become matted. Many owners peg them back at feed time.
Feeding: 1–1½ cans (14oz/400g size) of a branded meaty product, with biscuit added in equal part by volume.
Longevity: Can live into the teens.
Faults: Include prominent cheek bones.

Varieties: From left to right: golden, black, red, red and white, black and white, and blue.

Right: The American Cocker Spaniel, showing the slightly wavy coat and distinctive "trousers" characteristic of the breed.

Above: The English Springer Spaniel is one of the largest of the spaniels. Its name comes from the fact that it used to be used to flush out or "spring" game.

The Cocker stands 15½–16in (39–41cm) high, bitches 15–15½in (38–39cm). Weight approximately 28–32lb (12.7–14.5kg). Colors are various, but in self colors no white is allowed except on the chest.

The American Cocker is smaller than the English Cocker and has a silky, flat, or slightly wavy coat and distinctive "trousers." Bred in England, but developed in the United States where it is immensely popular, the American Cocker is also an excellent gundog and family pet and is debatably a more showy animal than the Cocker Spaniel. The American Cocker stands at 14–15in (36–39cm), bitches at 13–14in (34–36cm), and weighs about 26½lb (12kg). It occurs in a variety of colors. It is smaller than other hunting dogs, and is now usually kept as a pet.

143

The Foxhound

George Washington is credited with importing foxhounds from Britain and some fine specimens from France in 1785. We see the result of the cross-breeding of these English and French hounds in the American Foxhound.

Hounds stand 23in (58.5cm) high, bitches slightly less. No color is described as bad for a Foxhound. Attractive thought it may be, the Foxhound is entirely unsuitable as a household pet. Indeed, Foxhounds are not exhibited in the show ring in England except in a special hound show. They are, however, contenders in the show ring in America.

Foxhounds are invariably the property of a foxhunting pack and are described in couples, for example, "fifty couples of hounds," and the nearest they ever get to a domestic environment is in puppyhood, when they may be "puppy walked" by a member of the public.

The Foxhound is a descendant of the heavier St. Hubert Hound, which was brought to England by the Norman William the Conqueror and from another extinct hound, the Talbot. St. Hubert, or Hubertus,

Varieties: From top to bottom: black, fawn and white, tan and white, and red, black and white.

KEY FACTS

Character: Attractive, noisy hunter, which does not fit into a domestic environment.
Exercise: It is a hunter—enough said.
Grooming: Groom with a hound glove.
Feeding: Foxhounds are not reared on domestic pet food but are trencher-fed with horse flesh and a mash comprising oatmeal and known as "pudding."
Longevity: Good to average.
Faults: Include tail turned forward over back.

Below: The typical black, tan, and white coloring of the English Foxhound.

Above: The Foxhound does not fit easily into a domestic environment, and is usually only found in the packs owned by hunts.

Hounds took their name from the patron saint of hunters, associated in legend with an 8th-century bishop of Liège in Belgium.

The American Foxhound evolved from a pack of foxhounds taken to America by Robert Brooke in 1650.

The Beagle

Varieties: From left to right: tan and white, tan, gray and white, brown and white, and fawn and white.

KEY FACTS

Character: Happy, lovable, "naughty" little dog that probably shouldn't be kept as a pet, but often is.

Exercise: Revels in it.

Grooming: The Beagle's weatherproof coat requires little or no grooming.

Feeding: 1–1½ cans (14oz/400g size) of a branded meaty product, with biscuit added in equal part by volume.

Longevity: Can live into the teens.

Faults: Include destructiveness, disobedience, and slinking off.

The Beagle is an attractive small dog, with a penchant for wandering off, true to its hound instincts. It is not the most obedient of dogs. Indeed it can be noisy and a trifle tiresome, but it is nonetheless lovable. Many people will say that the right place for a Beagle is in a Beagle pack, but some have been devoted household pets for 14 years or more. They are good with children, and usually very healthy—great fun to go for a walk with!

Beagles are an ancient breed, written about at least since the end of the 15th century. They have hunted hare for centuries, but have been used against various quarry in different countries of the world: wild pigs in Sri Lanka, deer in Scandinavia, and jackals in the Sudan. They will retrieve, and in the USA they hunt by scent in Field Trials.

Standing a minimum of 13in (33cm), and no more than 16in (40cm) at the withers, the smart little Beagle can be any recognized hound color except white, but the top of its stern must be white.

The Irish Wolfhound

Despite the warning that the Irish Wolfhound can be fierce, the dog is generally a gentle giant; the one many people declare as their favorite and would love to own were it not for its size and feeding cost.

The national dog of Ireland, of which the Irish are naturally proud, this wolfhound was originally bred as a wolf hunter and is believed to have arrived from the continent with invading Celts in the 3rd century BC.

Few can relate without a tear the story of Gelert the Irish Wolfhound, presented as a gift to Llewellyn ap lorwerth, Prince of Wales, by King John of England in the early 1200s. One day Llewellyn went out hunting, leaving Gelert to look after his son. On his return he noticed that the dog's mouth was covered with blood and saw no sign of his son. On impulse, believing that the dog had killed his son, he slew the dog with his sword—whereupon he heard a cry and found nearby not only his unharmed son, but the body of a wolf. Llewellyn had a statue erected in memory of Gelert the Irish Wolfhound.

The Irish Wolfhound has a minimum height of 31in (79cm), bitches 28in (71cm). Its recognized colors are gray, brindle, red, black, pure white, fawn, wheaten, and steel gray.

KEY FACTS

Character: A gentle giant, good with children.
Exercise: Surprisingly does not need more than average exercise, but it does need room to spread itself.
Grooming: Brushing and some plucking. Exhibitors aim for the "natural" look with this majestic breed.
Feeding: At least 2½ cans (14oz/400g size) of a branded meaty product, with biscuit added in equal part by volume. This is a breed which needs stoking up with food in adolescence, so ask the breeder for a diet chart.
Longevity: Moderate to average.
Faults: Can be fierce when provoked.

Varieties: Top from left to right: wheaten, steel gray, black, and fawn; bottom from left to right: gray, white, red, and brindle.

The Bloodhound

Despite its association with detective stories and formidable trekking, the Bloodhound is a supremely gentle and affectionate animal which adores children. It makes an excellent pet provided you have room to accommodate it and neighbors who won't be averse to the sound of baying, which can be a trifle disconcerting.

Although a good watchdog, the Bloodhound is not a guard, and its instinct is to follow scent and find its quarry—not to attack. It does of course need a large amount of exercise and owners are recommended to join a Bloodhound Club which organizes events. Apart from trekking, Bloodhounds attract good entries in the show ring.

One of the oldest, purest breeds of hound, the Bloodhound is believed to have originated from the Mediterranean area, possibly Greece or Italy, before the Christian era. It was brought to England by William the Conqueror in 1066 and there the modern type was developed.

The Bloodhound stands 26in (66cm) high, bitches 24in (61cm), and may be black and tan, liver and tan (red and tan), and red, sometimes flecked with white. A small amount of white is permissible on the chest, feet, and tip of the tail.

Below: The Bloodhound has a formidable tracking ability, and needs a lot of exercise.

KEY FACTS

Character: Superlative tracker, good with children, and makes a good pet if you have room to accommodate it.

Exercise: A great deal.

Grooming: Use a hound glove daily.

Feeding; About 2–2½ cans (14oz/400g size) of a branded meaty product, with biscuit added in equal part by volume.

Longevity: Average.

Faults; Prone to torsion—a buildup of stomach gases. Be aware of this, and contact a veterinarian immediately if hound is in trouble.

Above: The Otterhound is probably descended from the Bloodhound, crossed with terriers and Griffons. Like the Bloodhound, it has an excellent nose, and is also good with children.

Varieties: From top to bottom: black and tan, liver, and red.

The Basenji

The Basenji is a delightful choice of pet. It is odourless and clean, and does not bark, giving only a kind of yodel; and is loyal, gentle, and affectionate. It is good with children.

The Basenji has many appealing features. It washes itself like a cat, for example, and has a forehead full of what look like concerned wrinkles.

An ancient breed, dogs of Basenji-type are depicted in carvings on the tombs of the Pharaohs, and it is thought that such dogs were presented as tribute by travelers from the upper reaches of the Nile.

The breed had almost disappeared from view until the mid-19th century when it was discovered by explorers in the southern Sudan and the Congo. Most of today's stock has been imported from the Sudan, and also from Liberia in West Africa. Rumor has it that the Basenji is also to be found in the Malaysian jungle and north of Kathmandu.

The Basenji's ideal height is 17in (43cm) at the

Varieties: From left to right: red and white, tan and white, black and white, and black.

withers, bitches 16in (40cm), and it comes in pure black-and-white, red-and-white, black, tan-and-white, and tan-and-white with tan melon pips and mask. The white should be on the feet, chest, and tail tips. White legs, blaze and a white collar are optional.

KEY FACTS

Character: Gentle, odorless, good with horses, friendly with children.
Exercise: Although a dog that essentially should be kept indoors with its owner—and not in an outside kennel—the Basenji was bred as a hunter, and enjoys open spaces.
Grooming: Use a hound glove.
Feeding: About 1½ cans (14oz/400g size) of a branded meaty product, with biscuit added in equal part by volume.
Longevity: Average.
Faults: Include dislike of rain, and the phenomenon of coming into season only once a year.

The Afghan Hound

The Afghan Hound enjoys immense popularity and attracts large entries in show classes. A loyal and affectionate animal, it needs gentle but firm handling if it is not to attempt dominance; at the same time it must be understood that this is a dog that does not respond to bullying. In other words, let the dog know you love it, but stay the boss.

The Afghan is an ancient breed and the story is often told that it was one of the animals chosen to be taken into Noah's Ark.

A papyrus discovered in Sinai dated around 3,000 BC was once thought to describe an early Afghan Hound. In any event, this Grayhound-type dog found its way to Afghanistan where its long, shaggy coat developed to protect it against the climatic conditions.

The Afghan Hound stands at 27–29in (68–74cm high), bitches 25–27in (63–69cm), and may be any color.

Varieties: Clockwise from top left: brown, fawn, cream, and tan and fawn.

The Dachshund

Above: The wire-haired Dachshund, which was created by crossing the smooth-haired with the Dandie Dinmont Terrier.

Below: The long-haired Dachshund, which was created by crossing with the Spaniel and a German breed called the Stoberhund.

The Dachshund comes into two sizes, standard and miniature, and in no less than three coats: smooth-haired, long-haired, and wire-haired. It also answers widely to the name of Teckel, Dackel, Dacksel, and Badger Hound (*Dachs* means "badger" in German), the latter description being most appropriate, for badger hunting was the purpose for which it was bred in its native Germany. What was wanted was a short-legged hound with a keen sense of smell, courage, and burrowing ability. The Dachshund is now famed for putting this latter ability to good use in its owner's backyards!

The Dachshund makes an excellent pet, is supremely affectionate, and generally likes children. However, it can be a little aggressive toward strangers and is a fine watchdog. It also has a very loud bark for its size—a real guard dog in miniature. Perhaps the only drawbacks to the breed are a tendency to disk trouble, if the dog is permitted to jump on and off chairs, and to being overweight.

KEY FACTS

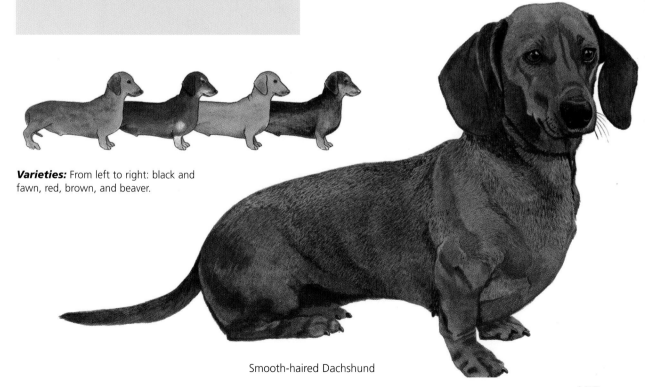

Character: Intelligent, lively, courageous. obedient and affectionate.

Exercise: Short, frequent walks help preserve the Dachshund's waistline.

Grooming: Use a hound glove and rub down with a soft brush. A stiff-bristled brush and a comb need to be used on the long- and wire-haired varieties.

Feeding: About ½ can (14oz/400g size) of a branded meaty product for the miniature; ¾–1 can maximum for the Standard, with biscuit added in equal part by volume.

Longevity: Some live into the teens.

Faults: Too much hair on the feet and hind dew claws.

Dachshunds have been around since at least the 16th century, having evolved from the oldest breeds of German hunting dogs, including the Bibarhund. The smooth-haired variety was the only one when the German Dachshund Club was formed in 1888. The wrinkled paws, then a characteristic of the breed, have been almost bred out. The wire-hair was designed by crossing with the Dandie Dinmont and other terriers, the long-hair by crossing the smooth-haired Dachshund with the spaniel and an obsolete German gundog called the Stoberhund.

All colors are allowed except in dapples, which should be evenly marked all over—no white permissible, save for a rather undesirable small patch on the chest. Black-and-tan and red are the most popular colors.

Ideal weights are: standards 20–26lb (9–12kg); miniatures 10lb (4.5kg).

Varieties: From left to right: black and fawn, red, brown, and beaver.

Smooth-haired Dachshund

153

The Grayhound

The Grayhound is a pure breed which does not appear to have changed a great deal since ancient Egyptian times, if we are to go by surviving carvings and paintings. It was among the first breeds to be trained to hunt. In more recent times it was highly prized among the nobility of Europe.

Although Grayhounds are bred as pets and for the show ring one tends to think of them predominantly as racers. Sadly, when that racing life is over, or should it end prematurely, this most docile of breeds often ends up in the

Below: The Pharaoh Hound, the earliest recorded domesticated breed, and a direct ancestor of the Grayhound.

Varieties: From top to bottom: fawn, brindle, blue and white, white, black, red, blue, and fallow.

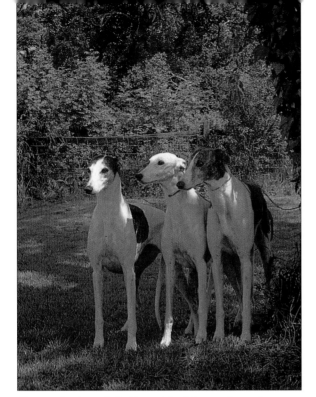

Above: Grayhounds that have retired from racing make excellent household pets. Once out of training, they do not need a lot of exercise.

KEY FACTS

Character: Has remarkable stamina and endurance, and is an adaptable, affectionate animal which makes a loyal and gentle pet.

Exercise: Normal, regular walks are sufficient, but never let a Grayhound (especially an ex-racer) off the lead in a public place or anywhere where there is livestock. Ex-racers need de-training, or they will chase anything that moves.

Grooming: Use a hound glove every day.

Feeding: 1½–2½ cans (14oz/400g size) of a branded meaty product, with biscuit added in equal part by volume. Grayhounds are used to sloppier foods than other breeds, and appreciate a thick slice of brown bread crumbled into milk at breakfast time and another drink of milk with a few biscuits at bedtime (most breeds enjoy bedtime biscuits as a treat).

Longevity: Can live as pets to a fairly ripe age.

Faults: Include a possible tendency to rheumatism and arthritis.

veterinary laboratory or at least in need of a pet home. Bearing it in mind that after a period of de-training they do make excellent pets, and do not, despite their size, take up much space in the home, preferring to deposit themselves on a comfortable couch in a corner, they are well worth considering if you want a big dog.

Grayhounds come in black, white, red, blue, fawn, fallow, brindle, or any of these colors broken with white. There is no weight standard, but their ideal height is 28–30in (71–76cm), bitches 27–28in (68–71cm).

If you are interested in giving a home to a "retired" Grayhound and are not thinking in terms of the show ring, it would be sensible to enquire at your nearest Grayhound Racing Club.

Left: The Saluki is another ancient hound. Like the Pharaoh Hound and Grayhound, it hunts by sight rather than scent. It is intelligent and gentle.

Index

iPage numbers in *italic* refer to illustrations and captions.

A

Aberdeen Terrier *see*
   Scottish Terrier
adult dog, feeding schedule 34
Affenpinscher 68, 76, *77*, 106, 108, *108*
Afghan Hound 40, 42, 71, 151, *151*
aggression 47, 152
ailments and injuries 54–5
Airedale Terrier 69, 122–3, *123*
Alaskan Malamute 29, 66, *90*
Alsatian Wolf Dog *see*
   German Shepherd dog
American Cocker Spaniel 70, *142*, 143
American Foxhound 11, 144–5
American Staffordshire Terrier 128–9
American Water Spaniel 136
anal glands 54
Anatolian Karabash 18
Anatolian Shepherd Dog 66, *97*
Anubis 9
Appenzell Sennenhund 82
Assistance dogs for the disabled 27
Australian Cattle Dogs 66
Australian Silky Terrier 68
Australian Terrier 69

B

bad breath 54
bad temper 78
barking, persistent 48
Basenji 48, 71, 150, *150*
Basset Fauve de Bretagne 71
Basset Hound 71, *71*, 100
bathing 43
Beagle 71, 146, *146*
Bearded Collie 66, *104–5*
Bedlington Terrier 69, 69
beds and bedding 32, *32, 33*
behavior, antisocial 48–9, 123
Belgian Shepherd Dog
   Groenendael 66, *103*
   Laekenois 66
   Malinois 66
   Tervueren 66
Bernese Mountain Dog 27, 67, 82–3, *83*
Best in Breed *41*

Bibarhund 153
Bichon Frisé 42, *68*
bitches
   gentleness of 30
   spaying of 56
   in whelp 58
Black and Tan Terrier *see*
   Old English Black-and Tan Terrier
      Bloodhound 71, 132, 132,
      134, 148, 148–9
boarding kennels 50–1
body positions, meanings of *47*
Border Collie 44, 67, *67*, 104, *104, 105*
Border Terrier 69, *124*
Borzoi 18, 71, *71*
Boston Terrier 66
Bouvier Des Flandres 67
Boxer *19*, 67, *94–5*, 94
Boykin Spaniel *see*
   American Water Spaniel
Brabant Bull-baiter 94
breathing, difficulty in hot weather 45,
   55, 106
breed rescue societies 30, 31, 61
breeding 57, *57*
   selective 10
breeds 64–5, *64–5*
   disappearing 14–15
   see also under individual
      breeds
Briard 67, *99*
Brindle Bull Terrier 127
Brittany 70
Broholmer 16
Brussels Griffon *see*
   Griffon Bruxellois
Bull Terrier 69, 69–70, 126–7, *126–7*
   miniature 69
bull-baiting *14*, 94
Bulldog *14–15*, 45, *60*, 66, 93
   lifespan 60
Bullmastiff 67, 93, *94*
burrowing 152
buying, do's and don'ts 31

C

Cairn Terrier 17, 69, 130, *131*
Canaan Dog 66
Caniche *see* Poodle
canine distemper 50, 52, 53

canine equipment *32*, 33
canine parvo virus 50, 53
canis familiaris, evolution of 8–9
canned food 34
carriage dogs 45, *45*, 76, 79
cars, dogs under control in *51*
castration 56, *56*
cattle dogs 100
Cavalier King Charles Spaniel 57, 68, 69,
   116–17, 116
Certificates of Pedigree *see*
   Pedigree certificates
Challenge Certificates 21
Championship Shows 40
championship systems,
   American and British 21
character *30*, 46
check chain *33*
Chesapeake Bay Retriever 70, 138
Chihuahua 18, 40, 45, 60, 69
   Long and Smooth coat 68, 118,
      118–19, 119
Chinese Crested Dogs 68, 109, *109*
Chinese spaniels *114*
choke chain 39
choking 54
choosing a dog 30–1
Chow Chow *11*, 21, 66, 75
claws 9
clipping 42
Clumber Spaniel 70
collapse 54
collars *33*, 39, 46
   wearing of 38
Collie (Rough and Smooth) 67, *104*,
   132, 132
combing 42
come command 38, *39*
companionship 28, *28*, 61, 116
   for children *46*
   for the elderly 27
coyote (prairie wolf) 11
cropping 43
crossbreeds *19*, 30
Crufts dog show 23, 28
cur 15
*Cynographia Curiosa oder
   Hundesbeschreibung,*
   Paullini 11

D

Dachshund 113, 152–3, *152–3*
  Long-haired 71, *152*
  Miniature 71
  Smooth-haired 71, *152, 153*
  Wire-haired 71, *152*
Dalmatian 45, *45*, 66, 79, *79*, 127
  spots 23
Dandie Dinmont Terrier 69, 111, 130,
  131, 152, 153
deafness, Dalmatians 79
Deerhound 71
diabetes 54
diarrhea 54
diet 24, 35, *35*
Dingo *10*, 11, *11*
distemper 50, 52, 53
Doberman 18, 40, 44, 67, 88–9, 88
docking 43
dog biscuit 34
"dog days" 13
dog foods *35*
Dog matches 41
Dog shows 41
dog training classes 39, 40, *46*, 128
dog training clubs 44, 86
dogs
  as draft animals 27, 82
  and the elderly 61
  elderly 60, 61
  and human moods 25
domestication 10–11
drinking water 34
drover's dogs 15

E

ears 43, *43*
  earache 54
  positions *23*
eczema 54
elderly dogs, care of 61
Elkhound 71, 100
English Mastiff 18
English Setter 70, 132, *133*
English Springer Spaniel 70, *143*
English Toy Terrier 68, *68*,120
Entlebuch Sennenhund 82
Essenes 13
Estrela Mountain Dog 67, *97*

F

Exemption dog shows (UK) 40
exercise 44–5, 44–5, 120, 123
  arrangements in boarding kennels
    50, 51
  and the bitch in whelp 58
  in winter 60
eyes 43, *43*
  injury to 55
eyesight, deterioration of 61

feeding charts 59
feet 19
  cut 54
  webbed *138*
Field Trials, Beagles 144
fighting dogs 74
Finnish Spitz 71, 80, *80*
fits 54
fleas 54
fox 8, *9*
Fox Terrier 17
  smooth and wire 69
fox-hunting 144
Foxhound 144–5, *144–5*
French Barbet 72
French Bulldog 40, 66, 78

G

gait 40
gaze hounds 71
Gelert legend 147
gentleness
  of bitches 30
  of Bloodhounds 148
German Mastiff 97
German Shepherd dog 11, 27, 44, 67,
102, *102–3*, 103
German Short-haired Pointer 70
German Smooth-haired Pinscher 113
German Spitz (Klein and Mittel) 66
German Whitehaired Pointer 70
Glen of Imaal Terrier 69, 124
Golden Retriever 57, 70, 133, 138, *139*
Gordon Setter 70, 132, *132*
Grayhound *11, 18*, 71, 154, *154–5*, 155
  retired, homes for 155
Great Dane 18, 58, 67, 86–7, *86–7*
  lifespan 60

Great Swiss Sennenhund 82
Greyfriars Bobby 28–9
Griffon *149*
  Brabançon 106, *107*
  Brussels 42, 68, *106, 107*
grooming 30, 42–3
  equipment *42*
groups 66–71
guard dogs 12–13, 26, 69, 84, 88, 93,
  97, 98, 99, 134
guarding instinct 24, 47, 88, 103
guide dogs for the blind 26, *27*, 60, 94,
  102, 138, 141
gundogs *see* sporting dogs

H

Hamiltonstovare 71
handling classes 40, *40*
health care 52–3
hearing, deterioration of 61
hearing dogs for the deaf *26–7, 26*
heart attacks 55
heat stroke 55
heel command *38–9*
hepatitis, viral 50, 53
herding dogs 67, 99–105
hip dysplasia 96, 103
holy dogs 12–13
home-finding 59
hotels, accepting pets 51
Hottentot Hunting Dog *57*
hounds 71, 144–55
house-training 36–7
Hovawart 67
Hungarian Puli 67
Hungarian Vizsla 70, *134*
  presentation of *41*
Hungarian Water Hound 72

I

Ibizan Hound 71
incontinence 55
injury *see* ailments and injury
inoculations 52–3
  proof of 50
  records 52, 59
insurance 49,59
intelligence 24–5, 72, 119, 134,
  135, 142

Inuit Dog 10–11, *11*, 67
Irish Red and White Setters 28, *132*
Irish Setter 47, 70, 132, *132*
    litter size 57
Irish Terrier 69, 124
Irish Water Spaniel *see under* Spaniel
Irish Wolfhound 18, 71, 147, *147*
Italian Greyhound 68, 113, 120, *120, 121*
Italian Spinone 70

J

Jack Russell Terrier *24*, 69
jackal 8, *9*, 11
Japanese Akita 66
Japanese Chin 68, *115*
Japanese Spitz 66, 80, *80*
Jones Terrier *see* Norwich Terrier

K

Keeshond 66
Kennel Club (American) 129
Kennel Club (United Kingdom) 18, 125
kennel cough 55
    inoculation against 50
kennels
    indoor 32, *33*, 49
    outdoor 33, 98
Kerry Blue Terrier 69
key words (training) 24
King Charles Spaniel 68, 116, *117*
Komondor 67, 98, *98*

L

Labrador Retriever 60, 70, 133, 140–1, *140–1*
Lakeland Terrier *122*
Lama's Mastiff 75
lamb clip 42
Lancashire Heeler 67
Landseer, Sir Edwin 92
lap dogs 11, 68
Large Munsterlander 70
leash, use of 38, 106
leash training *38*
leash vs. harness 32
leashes *33*
legs, broken 54
Leonberger 66
leptospirosis 50, 53
Lhaso Apso 66, *66,114*
lifespan 60, 87
limp 55
lion clip (cut) 17, 42, 73

litter size 9, 57, *59*
Lowchen 17, 68
loyalty 24, *29*, 83, 84
Lundehund 16

M

Maltese 68
Maltese Terrier *68,* 111, *111*
man-and-dog fights 47
Manchester Terrier 18, *68*, 88, *89*
mange 55
Maremma Sheepdog 67
Mastiff *11*, 44, 67, *67*, 86, 93
    German 97
mating *57*
    unusual, fertile 8
mealtime tips 35
meat, fresh vs. branded pet food 34
Metempsychosis 12
miacis 8, *8*
Miniature Pinscher (Min Pin) 68, 108, 113, *113*
misalliance 55
Molossus hounds 86, 94
mongrels 19, 19, 30
muzzling *47*

N

nails 43, *43*
Neapolitan Mastiff 67, *86*
neutering 56
Newfoundland 29, 67, 92, 138
nipping 100
Nome Serum Run 27
Nordic (Norbotten) Spitz 80
Norfolk Terrier 69, 24–5, *125*
Norwegian Buhund 67, 80, *81*
Norwich Terrier 69, 124–5, *125*
nutritional requirements 34

O

obedience 38, 39, 76, 102, 104, 122, 136
odorless dogs 150
Old English Black-and-Tan Terrier 111, 128
Old English Sheepdog 42, 67, 99, *99*
Open shows 40
Otterhound 71, 122, *149*
overheating in warm
    weather 106
overshot jaw *22*

P

pack behavior 24, 25
pack leaders 9, 25, 25
Papillon 18, 68, *119*
Pariah dogs 11, *11*
parvo virus 50, 53
Patrol dogs 26
Pedigree Certificates 20–1, 21, 22, 31, 59
Pekingese 11, 44, 68, 114–15, *115*
Petit Basset Griffon 71
Pharaoh Hound 9, 9, 71, *154*
Phu Doc dogs *10*
pills, administration of *53*
Pinscher 67, 113
    see also Miniature Pinscher
Pit Bull Terrier 128–9
play *29*, 46
play-fighting 46
plucking 42
Podengo *16*, 16–17
Pointer 70, *70*, 88, 132, 134
points of the dog 20
poisoning 55
police dogs 84, *85*, 123, 134, 141
Poltalloch (Roseneath) Terrier 130
Pomeranian 14, 44, 68, 112, *112*
Poodles 42, 60
    miniature, standard, and toy 66, 68, 72, *72–3*, 73, 136
pooper scooper 49
Portuguese Warren Hound
    see Podengo
Portuguese Water Dog 17, *17*, 67
Powder Puffs *see* Chinese Crested Dog
praise, necessity for 36
Prefix 20
Pro-Dogs Active Therapy Dogs 27, *27*
Pug 68, 106, *107*
Puli *see* Hungarian Puli
puppies buying, do's and don'ts 31
    equipment for 32–3, *32–3*
    exercise 45
    feeding schedule 34
    health check *31*
    house-training 36–7, *36–7*
    inoculation of 52–3
    weaning 59
puppy walking 144
pure breed 18, *19*, 22, 30
Pyrenean Mountain Dog 67, 97

R

Red Setter *see* Irish Setter
Retriever
    Curly-coated 70, 136, *137*, 138

Flat-coated 70, *137, 138, 141*
see also Chesapeake Bay Retriever;
    Golden Retriever;
    Labrador Retriever
retrieving 46
Rhodesian Ridgeback *57*, 71
Ringcraft classes 40, 40
road accidents 55
Rottweiler 18, 27, 44, 67, 84–5,
    84–5, 88
Rough Collie *104*
Russian Owtscharka 99

S

Saluki 9, 9, 12, *13*, 71, 155
Samoyed *10*, 11, 67, *91*, 100
Sanction shows 40
scent hounds 71
Schipperke 60, 66, *66*
Schnauzer 66
    giant 67, *76*, 77
    miniature 66, 76, *77*
    standard 76, *77*
Scottish Terrier 69, 70, 130
Sealyham Terrier 69
search and rescue dogs 26, 90, 102
Setters 70, *132*, 132–3, *133*
Shar-Pei 16, 66, 74, *74*
sheepdog *see* Border Collie;
    shepherd dog
sheepdog trials 104
shepherd dogs 11, 12–13, 67, 82, *97*,
    104–5, *104–5*
Shetland Sheepdog 67
Shih Tzu 66
shock 55
short-nosed breeds,
    difficulties in hot weather 45, 106
show dogs 20–1, 22–3
show stance 40
showing 40–1
    preparation for 42
Siberian Husky 67, 90, *90, 91*
Siberian Wild Dog *10*, 11
sit command 38–9, 38
skin folds 74
Skye Terrier 69, *69*, 111
sled dog racing 90
"sleeve" Pekes *see* Pekingese
Sloughi 71
Sniffer dogs *26–7, 26*, 141
Soft-coated Wheaten Terrier 69
Spaniel 68, 70, *70*
    American Cocker 70, *142*, 143
    Clumber 70
    Cocker 70, *142*, 142–3

English Springer 70, *143*
Field 70
Springer 132
Sussex 70
Tibetan 66, *114, 115*
Welsh Springer 70
see also Chinese Spaniel;
    Water Spaniel
Spanish Pointer 132
spaying 56, *56*
Spitz breeds *11*, 66, 71, 75, 80, *90*, 112
sporting dogs 45, 70, 132–43.
Staffordshire Bull Terrier 69–70, 128,
    128–9, 129
standards, Kennel Clubs 22
status dogs 12
stay command *38–9, 38*
Stoberhund *152*, 153
St. Bernard 18, 29, 67, *96*, 96–7
St. Hubert Hound 134, 144
stripping 42, 123
Swedish Vallhund 67
swimming 92
Swiss Mountain dogs 82
    see also Bernese Mountain Dog

T

Tahltan Bear Dog 16
tail positions *22*
Talbot Hound 144
Tartar Dog *see* Chow Chow
Teckel *see* Dachshund
teeth 43, *43*
television, effect of 99
temperament 47
temperature 55
terriers *11*, 69–70, 122–31, *149*
third party insurance 49
Tibetan Mastiff 67, 93, 97
Tibetan Spaniel 66, *114, 115*
Tibetan Terrier 66
tie *57*
toes 8–9
tomarctus 8, 8
totemism 12
Toxocara canis 52
toy breeds 58
toy dogs 57, 68, 106–21
    at shows 40, *40*
    exercise 44–5
toy Poodle *see* Poodle, toy 33, *33*
tracking 46, 148, *148*
training 24–5, 38–9, 93
training parks, accepting pets
    51, *51*
transfer form 20, 31, 59

Turkish Shepherd Dog *see* Anatolian
    Karabash
turnspit dogs 14–15

U

undershot jaw *22*, 94, *94*
utility dogs *see* non-sporting dogs

V

vaccination *see* inoculation
Vendéen 71
veterinary examination,
    older dogs 61
Viszla *see* Hungarian Viszla

W

walking, position for 38
watchdogs 12, 15, 47, 152
    see also guard dogs
Water Spaniels, Irish and American 70,
    132, 136, *136, 137*
weaning 59
weight-hauling contests 29
Weil's Disease 53
Weimaraner 70, 134–5, *135*
Welsh Corgi 17
    Cardigan 11, 67,*101*, 100
    Pembroke 67, 100, *100,101*
Welsh Springer Spaniel 70
Welsh Terrier 69, *122*
West Highland White Terrier 57, 69, 70,
    130, 130–1
whelping 58
whelping box 58
Whippet 71, *121*
White English Terrier 127
wolf 8, *9*, *11*, *103*
Wood Green Animal Shelter *31*
work, as play 26
working dogs 67, 82–105
    exercise 44
worming 52, 55, 59
wrinkles 74

Y

yappiness 48, 80, 106
yard, fenced 32
yodeling 48
Yorkshire Terrier 18, 44, 60, *60*, 68, 69,
    110, *110–11*, 111

Credits

KEY T = TOP
B = BELOW
C = CENTRE
L = LEFT
B = BELOW
p.2: Marc Henrie. p.6: Marc Henrie. p.7: Marc Henrie. p.8: C.M. Dixon. p.9: Solitaire Photographic. p.10: T. Anne Marie Bazalik; B. Australian Overseas Information Service, London. p.12: C.M. Dixon. p.13: Marc Henrie. p.14: C.M. Dixon. p.15: E.T. Archive. p.16: Marc Henrie. p.17: Marc Henrie. p.18: Marc Henrie. p.19: T. Marc Henrie; B. Marc Henrie. p.21: Quarto Publishing plc. p.23: Marc Henrie. p.24: L. Ardea, London; R. Norvia Behling. p.25: Norvia Behling. p.26: L. Marc Henrie; R. Marc Henrie. p.27: L. Marc Henrie; R. Paul Forester. p.28–29: Solitaire Photographic. p.30: Marc Henrie. p.31: Wood Green Animal Shelters. p.32: Solitaire Photographic. p.33: Marc Henrie. p.37: Norvia Behling. p.39: Marc Henrie. p.40: T. Solitaire Photographic; B. Marc Henrie. p.41: Solitaire Photographic. p.44: L. Norvia Behling; R. Marc Henrie. p.45: J.S. Library International. p.46: Anne Marie Bazalik. p.47: C.M. Dixon: B. Kent & Donna Dannen. p.48: Norvia Behling. p.49: T. Kent & Donna Dannen; B. Marc Henrie. p.50: L. Marc Henrie; R. Kent & Donna Dannen. p.51: T. Marc Henrie; B. Solitaire Photographic. p.52: Marc Henrie. p.53: Solitaire Photographic. p.57: Anne Marie Bazalik. p.58: Solitaire Photographic. p.59: L. Marc Henrie; R. Marc Henrie. p.60: T. Marc Henrie; B. Marc Henrie. p.61: Marc Henrie. p.62: Agnes Leith. p.63: David C. Bitters. p.64: L. Marc Henrie; R. Ronald R. Domb. p.65: T. Marc Henrie; B. Marc Henrie. p.66: T. Marc Henrie; B. Solitaire Photographic. p.67: T. Solitaire Photographic; B. Brian A. Lewis. p.68: T. Solitaire Photographic; B. Solitaire Photographic. p.69: T. Marc Henrie; B. Marc Henrie. p.70: Solitaire Photographic (T & C). p.71. Marc Henrie (T & C). p.73: T. Solitaire Photographic; B. Anne Marie Bazalik. p.76: Marc Henrie. p.77: Solitaire Photographic. p.80: L. Marc Henrie; R. Solitaire Photographic. p.81: Marc Henrie. p.83: T. Marc Henrie; B.A.E. Linscott. p.85: L. Marc Henrie; R. Solitaire Photographic. p.86: T. Marc Henrie; B. Marc Henrie. p.89: T. Marc Henrie; B. Solitaire Photographic. p.90: Marc Henrie. p.91: Marc Henrie; p.92: T. Marc Henrie; B. Kent & Donna Dannen. p.93: Kent & Donna Dannen. p.95: T. Marc Henrie; B. Julie O'Neil-Photo/Nats. p.96: T. Marc Henrie; B. Anne Marie Bazalik. p.97: Marc Henrie. p.102: T. Julie O'Neill Photo/Nats. B. Marc Henrie. p.104: T. David M. Stone—Photo/Nats; B. Marc Henrie. p.105: Solitaire Photographic. p.106: L. Solitaire Photographic; R. Marc Henrie. p.111: T. Solitaire Photographic; B. Solitaire Photographic. p.114: Marc Henrie. p.115: Solitaire Photographic. p.117: T. Marc Henrie; B.Marc Henrie. p.118: Marc Henrie. p.119: Marc Henrie. p.121: Anne Marie Bazalik. p.122: T. Marc Henrie; B. Marc Henrie. p.124: Marc Henrie. p.125: Marc Henrie. p.126: Marc Henrie. p.127: Solitaire Photographic. p.128: Marc Henrie. p.131: T. Marc Henrie; B. Marc Henrie. p.132: Marc Henrie. p.133: Solitaire Photographic. p.134: Marc Henrie. p.134: Marc Henrie. p.137: Solitaire Photographic. p.138: Solitaire Photographic. p.139: Anne Marie Bazalik. p.141: T. Solitaire Photographic; B. Marc Henrie. p.142: Marc Henrie. p.143: Marc Henrie. p.144–145 Solitaire and Marc Henrie p.148: T. Marc Henrie; B. Marc Henrie. p.152: T. Marc Henrie; B. Marc Henrie. p.154: Marc Henrie. p.155: L. Spectrum Colour Library; R. Marc Henrie.

Quarto extends its special thanks to Pet World, Bromley Road, London, for the loan of equipment used in some photographs.